MOREISH

52 SHORT STORIES,
SERMONS AND STUDIES
GIVING YOU PLENTY OF
FOOD FOR THOUGHT

MOREISH

ISHMAEL

CWR **Applying God's Word**
to everyday life and relationships

Copyright © Ian Smale 2013

Published 2013 by CWR, Waverley Abbey House, Waverley Lane, Farnham, Surrey GU9 8EP, UK.

CWR is a Registered Charity – Number 294387 and a Limited Company registered in England – Registration Number 1990308.

The right of Ian Smale to be identified as the author of this work has been asserted by him in accordance with the Copyright, Designs and Patents Act 1988, sections 77 and 78.

All rights reserved. No part of this publication may be reproduced, stored in a retrieval system, or transmitted, in any form or by any means, electronic, mechanical, photocopying, recording or otherwise, without the prior permission in writing of CWR.

For list of National Distributors visit www.cwr.org.uk/distributors

Unless otherwise indicated, all Scripture references are from the Holy Bible: New International Version (NIV), copyright © 1979, 1984 by Biblica (formerly International Bible Society). Other versions as marked: *Message*: Scripture taken from THE MESSAGE, copyright © 1993, 1994, 1995, 1996, 2000, 2001, 2002. Used by permission of NavPress Publishing Group. Amplified: Scripture quotations taken from the Amplified® Bible, copyright © 1954, 1958, 1962, 1964, 1965, 1987 by The Lockman Foundation. Used by permission (www.Lockman.org). New Revised Standard Version Bible, copyright © 1989 National Council of the Churches of Christ in the United States of America. Used by permission. All rights reserved.

The poem 'Why?' by Gordon Bailey (*Mix and Match* 1999: ISBN 0 9535889 0 4) is used with permission.

Concept development, editing, design and production by CWR

Printed in the UK by Page Brothers

ISBN: 978-1-78259-018-7

Introduction

Following on from my last book for CWR, *A Year According to Ishmael*, which had 365 daily readings, I wanted to write a book of slightly more in-depth weekly readings. So, here it is: *MoreIsh*.

As well as looking at some well-known stories, characters and passages from the Bible, I've also selected a few very obscure ones, which would rarely be preached on from a pulpit! As you'd expect, it's written in typical Ish style: easy to read, with a balance of tongue-in-cheek humour and thought-provoking challenge.

I've also spent quite a time researching some historical and cultural detail, which I'm hoping will help readers understand the Scriptures better. As well as providing a little more simple Bible knowledge for those who are not intellectuals or theologians, my prayer is, as always, that this will not be just an enjoyable read but that God will speak to and encourage all who read it.

Acknowledgements

A big thank you to …

All the Bible commentaries and Bible teachers from whom I gleaned the biblical and historical knowledge to help me write this book.

Naomi Sheldrake, who was being treated for leukaemia and yet, in between chemotherapy treatments, still managed to help sort out my tenses and punctuation.

The Rev Dr Anthony Kane, the cathedral theologian, who checked the biblical contents of this book.

Huw Spanner for his sensitivity, knowledge and thoroughness in the overall editing of this book.

The Chichester Cathedral clergy, and especially the Precentor, Tim Scofield, and Dean, Nicholas Frayling, for allowing me to preach fifty per cent of these studies in the cathedral – and, of course, thanks to the congregation who had to listen to them.

Dr Adam and Gloria Bradford and Ian and Jane Cheal for their continued friendship and continuing support for my ministry.

And, of course, my fantastic wife, Irene, who allowed me to shut myself away for many hours to write it.

To find out more about Ish: **www.ishmaeldirect.com**

To contact Ish, email ishmael@ishm(x)ael.org.uk

Contents

Time is on our side!

KEY VERSE 'There's an opportune time to do things, a right time for everything on the earth: A right time for birth and another for death.' Ecclesiastes 3:1–2 (The Message)

'TIME IS ON my side,' Mick Jagger sang in 1965. But would he still say that today, I wonder. I don't know about you but, although I'm sure I look older, I don't actually feel any older than I did a year ago – or maybe even ten years ago! But I have noticed that the older I get, the more quickly the years seem to pass by.

For nearly forty years my role as a travelling evangelist and musician has meant that my life has been ruled by the calendar and the clock. My diary has been my most valuable possession – after my Bible, of course! All the places I'm meant to be are written in it, and all the times I have to be there. But in April a few years ago I was experiencing a typical crazy week. It began with an exhausting day finishing recording an album, and then I drove down to Falmouth for a friend's birthday party. It was a long drive to Cornwall from Chichester, and somehow it seemed an even longer drive home. I felt tired.

Next, my diary dictated that I must drive up to Lowestoft for the Caister Bible Week. Not only were Irene and I booked to speak, I was keen to go as I knew that the people there would be from the much 'higher' end of the Church of England than I was used to and I was eager to see what went on. The day after we got back, I had to help my son Dan move to London, but I was not a lot of help as I had no energy left.

The next day was a Sunday but my diary informed me that it was not a day of rest: I had to be up at the crack of dawn to be interviewed by Southern Counties Radio in Brighton. After that, I had to drive to a studio in Eastbourne to drop off the master CD of the new album for duplication. The journey home from Eastbourne was a nightmare. It was the one day that year we had a snowstorm and I got stuck in a major traffic jam, mainly due to the fact that southerners don't know how to drive in snow!

On the next day, the Monday, my life changed. Having had very little warning that I was even ill, I discovered that without immediate medication I would die within days from leukaemia! For the foreseeable future, I would be going nowhere outside of a hospital ward. And I was instructed to clear my diary for the rest of the year. As I lay in that hospital bed, staring at four walls, a ceiling and an annoying clock, I realised that time for me had stopped. Now, time meant nothing.

For many of us today, timing is everything. So often we get stressed over silly things. I've stood in a queue outside our (now solitary) post office waiting for it to open. As the moment approached, I've seen people become agitated, and even angry, if the doors didn't open on the stroke of nine. Now, of course, we get stressed at the amount of time we have to queue *inside* the post office. Likewise, we are very intolerant if we arrange to meet someone and they are a few minutes late. They'd better have a good reason! And, of course, although many a church service fails to start on time, it's vital that it *ends* on time. After the final benediction, there are important things we must do and places we must be!

But time is not the same to God as it is to us. As the psalmist reminds us in Psalm 90:4, a thousand years in His sight are but as yesterday. Isaac Watts used Psalm 90 as the basis for his famous hymn 'O God, Our Help in Ages Past':

'A thousand ages in Thy sight
Are like an evening gone;
Short as the watch that ends the night
Before the rising sun.'

God has all eternity in which to work. It is only against the background of eternity that things appear in their true proportions and with their real value. Man is mortal. Human beings die and any hope for life beyond death depends wholly on God and not on us.

However, God is different. 1 Timothy 6:16 informs us that He alone is immortal. He is without a beginning or an ending. He dwells in eternity. We have to try and get our heads around the fact that eternity is not just extended time, it is existence above and separate from time. So, it follows that if a thousand years is as a single day to God, we can never accuse Him of being late in anything He does. In His sight, the whole universe is only a few days old!

God is never limited by our sense of timing. The Old Testament often shows us that God is never in a hurry, but (as I have explained) actually it is impossible for Him to be. I have heard Christians complain that He always seems to answer prayer at the eleventh hour; but God does not know an eleventh hour. He knows only perfect timing. It was not God's timing for me to go and be with Him yet, and so I am still here. God still has a purpose for me here on earth, just as He has for all of us.

Every day is a gift of God's mercy. This means that every day we are alive, there is more opportunity for us to get closer to God and (just as important) to share His love with those around us who don't yet know Him. So …

Let's try not to waste time.

Let's make the most of the time allowed to us.

Let's make the most of every day.

For us believers, time *is* on our side!

Leper skin

KEY VERSE

'If that animal blood and the other rituals of purification were effective in cleaning up certain matters of our religion and behavior, think how much more the blood of Christ cleans up our whole lives, inside and out.' Hebrews 9:13 (*The Message*)

IF I'VE JUST sat through a very long, boring sermon – not in your church, of course! – I often remark: 'That sermon made *Ben Hur* seem like an epic.' But of course the 212-minute, fifteen million dollar movie (back in 1959!) *was* an epic. The nine-minute chariot race has become one of the most famous sequences in cinema history, but for me two of the most memorable scenes are when Ben Hur's mother and sister contract leprosy and then later are miraculously healed, just at the point when Jesus is crucified. But that's just a movie.

Leprosy was rife in the time of Jesus, though. It's a disease that can reduce a human being to a hideous ruin. In New Testament times, any skin disease rendered the sufferer unclean and that's why Jesus told His disciples to heal the sick and 'cleanse' lepers (Matt. 10:8).

Lepers:

- were banned from society;
- had to live outside the camp;
- had to walk around with torn clothes and shaved heads and keep their top lips covered.

Worst of all, perhaps, they were not allowed to go near anyone, including family and friends. If someone came too close, they had to shout out 'Unclean!' Not only were they barred from all normal social interaction, lepers were also excluded from the assembly of God. People didn't feel sorry for lepers, they felt revulsion. Lepers were unclean, contagious and condemned.

British society had a similar attitude in the Middle Ages. The church simply applied the Mosaic law. The priest put on his stole and, crucifix in hand, led the leper into the church and read the burial service over them.

The leper was pronounced dead even though they were still alive! From then on, they had to wear a black garment that marked them out to everyone. They must never enter a church building, though they were allowed to look in through the 'leper squint' that was cut in many church walls. They had to bear not only the physical effects of the disease but also the mental anguish and heartbreak of being completely banished from human society.

There was no cure for leprosy back then – but if someone had some other skin disease that had been mistaken for leprosy and was cured, they had to undergo a complicated ceremony of restoration as described in Leviticus 14 before they could be pronounced clean. This included being examined by a priest.

Jesus came to reverse this situation. Part of His task on earth was to see that lepers were healed, restored and reintegrated. In Mark 1:40, a leper approaches Jesus but instead of 'Unclean!' he shouts: 'Lord, if You are willing You can make me clean.' 'If You are willing' is an interesting remark. It doesn't mean 'If You are in a good mood'. It means 'If it is not out of line with God's purposes'. He seems to have no doubt about Jesus' power and submits to His will.

A little aside …

God has the ability to heal everyone but, hard as it is to understand, we need to recognise that God also has the right not to heal everyone. Difficult as it sometimes is, we need to submit to His will and accept that we do not know what is best, only He does. Some of my charismatic friends claim that 'God is always willing' and always wants to heal everyone, but Jesus does not correct the leper when he makes the remark 'If you are willing …'

At the other extreme, some of my friends who believe that the miraculous gifts of the Holy Spirit ceased early in Church history find it hard to believe that God *ever* wants to heal anyone today. To me, that is just as unbiblical.

In Chichester Cathedral, we have our own saint, called Richard. Legend tells us that this man of God performed many miracles and supernatural healings. I wonder how many people really believe the stories that are told about him? Personally, I don't find it hard to believe that, if Saint Richard was a man who both knew God's will and believed in His power, of course he was capable of doing mighty wonders under the anointing of the Holy Spirit.

Anyway, back to our story.

Now, remember, lepers were not allowed to approach people. The newly recruited disciples, who have only just met Jesus, must have felt very uncomfortable with this leper intruding into their space and must have felt the urge to start throwing stones at him as they had every right to do. But Jesus responds with compassion. Most translations note that He feels sorry for the leper, but some early manuscripts say that He was 'angry' rather than compassionate. Whether compassionate or angry, this point is important. Jesus does heal out of compassion, but there is also a place for righteous indignation at the effects of disease on people.

I get a little angry on my regular chaplaincy visits to our local hospital when I see patients suffering and in great pain from cancer or other diseases. I think we all get angry when we see sickness harming or even destroying the ones we love. This anger makes us want, as the theologian Tom Wright says, 'to put things to right'.

Whether out of compassion or anger, Jesus comes to reverse the curse of the effects of sickness and isolation caused by leprosy. Again to the shock of His disciples, Jesus reaches out His hand and touches the leper. This was something that was forbidden because leprosy was thought to be highly contagious and by touching the leper Jesus is making Himself unclean. Two things could happen now: either Jesus could catch leprosy or the leper could catch Jesus …

Of course, there can be only one outcome: the leper is wonderfully healed. Jesus tells the leper firmly to keep quiet about his healing, except for showing himself to the priest (which will allow him once again to join the assembly of God in the synagogue and the Temple). Why would He say this?

At this point, Jesus does not need or want publicity. His priority is His mission. He is more concerned with doing His messianic task than promoting His messianic status. He wants to be able to move among the towns and cities of Galilee freely. In fact, though, He ends up having to find refuge from the crowds in desolate and deserted places. From now on, everyone will crowd around Him to see a miracle rather than to actually listen to the words He has to say.

This is understandable. Even today, we can be far more interested in what Jesus can do for us and the blessings we can receive from Him than in wanting to learn from His teachings. Christians will flock to a concert, worship event or service majoring on 'signs and wonders' but, sadly, Bible studies just don't seem to have the same attraction.

Clearly, the leper disobeys Jesus. I'm sure that in his excitement his intentions are good. He wants everyone to know what this Jesus has done and rejoice with him. But just because his intentions are good doesn't mean that his actions are right. Still, the forgiving and compassionate Jesus makes the leper clean.

As an evangelist, part of the purpose of my life is to try to remind people gently that as we are all sinners, we all desperately need Jesus to heal, restore, forgive and cleanse us.

Because of Jesus, the leper is made clean and starts a brand new life. Because of Jesus, believers, too, are made clean. All their sins are forgiven and they, too, are able to start a brand new life. But there is one big difference. The leper is told not to tell anyone. The believer has been given the opposite instruction. So, let's do as Jesus commanded and go into all the world and preach His good news to all creation!

Don't worry, be happy

KEY VERSE

'Therefore I tell you, stop being perpetually uneasy (anxious and worried) about your life.' Matthew 6:25 (Amplified Bible)

THE VERY TALENTED Bobby McFerrin is famous for his amazing singing technique, which includes an unusually large vocal range of four octaves. But what really brought him fame was a song called 'Don't Worry, Be Happy'. Personally, I find this song rather irritating, but I won't be too detrimental about it as it may be one of your favourites! It's a nice sentiment, though – stop worrying and be happy – but sadly the song gives no hint of how someone *can* stop worrying. However, back in 1988 it obviously did make a lot of Americans happy because it was a number one hit in the US charts for two weeks.

Here in the UK, we seem to enjoy hearing about people's worries more. We even laugh at them. In one episode of the classic comedy *Fawlty Towers*, Sybil Fawlty talks about her mother:

'My mother is a worrier. She has morbid fears, really. Vans are one of them. Rats, doorknobs, birds, heights, open spaces, confined spaces.

'It's very difficult to get a space right for her, really.

'Footballs, bicycles, cows – and she's always worried about men following her. Oh yes, and death.'

A biblical definition of worry or anxiety might be 'a care that brings disruption to the personality and mind'. It pulls us in a different direction and distracts us.

Just to clarify, worry should not be mixed up with concern. Every day, I am concerned for the safety of my two sons living in London, for my daughter and her family – and, of course, for Irene, as she has to live with me! Each morning, I pray about these concerns and try to leave them in the Lord's hands.

While on earth, Jesus, too, seemed concerned about things, and certainly Jerusalem and His disciples. That is why He prayed to His Father about them. Concern for someone else's welfare, health or happiness is a good quality and necessary for righteousness. But worry is different.

In Matthew 6, we read the Sermon on the Mount, in which Jesus passes on to His disciples the message He wants them to spread around the world. Someone once called it 'the ordination address to the Twelve'. Jesus tells them they must trust God for their basic needs and seek His kingdom first. There is no need for them to be anxious or worry.

Growing up in a Christian community, I saw from a child's point of view what it is like when everyone shares everything. No one was richer or poorer than anyone else. I genuinely saw people who had no worries about their daily needs. Food was mainly provided from the 11-acre smallholding my father oversaw. Drink was plentiful, although – unless someone had a secret stash somewhere – I think it was all alcohol-free; and clothes (and fashion) were not an issue. Nobody seemed to care about image in the 1950s, especially if you were living in a small Sussex village.

When Jesus was speaking to His disciples, He was addressing a community that had one, common purse, with Judas as the treasurer. Although later on Judas' reputation went downhill, we must assume that when Jesus first gave him the job he was honest and shared the money around equally.

It is not the same with believers today. If I were to say to a wealthy Christian, 'Jesus says not to worry about the day's necessities,' they might honestly reply: 'I don't.' There are many rich people who in truth have never really had to trust God for any material things. But if I travel to some city suburb and meet a Christian with a family to support who has just been made redundant and I say to them, 'Jesus says not to worry,' they will probably say they can't help but worry!

I could remind them of the message of Matthew 6: 'Trust God to provide your food, drink and clothing. If He looks after flowers and birds, how much more will He look after you and your family?' But even though they might want to believe those words, I still think they might worry. It hardly seems fair that some will feel guilty over this scripture while others never will.

So, are worry and anxiety actually sinful? Some of my more extreme fundamentalist, evangelical friends would definitely suggest that they are. They might also accuse a sick person of lacking in faith if they took prescribed medicines or remained ill after prayer and the laying on of hands. However, I would question just how many of my friends who preach this really believe it and are actually living worry-free lives.

Worry is a common human emotion, but it is a negative one. There is no way we can enjoy 'life to the full' if we allow negative thinking to dominate our minds. We must try to think positively, and to spend more time counting our blessings. Peter tells us that when we are feeling worried we should 'cast all our anxiety upon' Jesus. It does seem to be the obvious and right thing to do, but our ever-gracious Lord also understands our human weaknesses and knows that even after we have prayed about our worries we often still feel a little anxious.

Anacreon, the ancient Greek poet, wrote: 'When I drink wine, my worries go to sleep.' No doubt when he was sober his worries woke up again. Perhaps a more permanent solution would be to follow Mary C Crowley's advice: 'Every evening I turn my worries over to God. He's going to be up all night anyway.'

Was Jesus ever anxious? Matthew, Mark and Luke all tell us that just before His crucifixion, Jesus fell to the ground three times, saying: 'My Father, if it is possible, may this cup be taken from Me. Yet Your will be done.' Luke follows this by saying that 'being in an agony [of mind], He prayed all the more earnestly and intently, and His sweat became like great clots of blood dropping down upon the ground' (Amplified Bible). Modern research confirms that under extreme stress this can happen. A doctor friend also informs me that medical evidence suggests that at this moment Jesus' heart-lining may have split. If that was the case, from then on His death was just a matter of time, Roman nails or not.

Of course, being human we can never understand what the Son of God was going through at that point; but Jesus was in such a state that an angel arrived to strengthen Him. Did Jesus feel some form of anxiety as He knew He was soon to suffer horrific torture and be separated from His Father for the first time ever? We don't know – but one thing we can be sure of is that He committed no sin.

Philippians 4:7 reminds us (in *The Message*): 'Don't fret or worry. Instead of worrying, pray.

'Let petitions and praises shape your worries into prayers, letting God know your concerns.

'Before you know it, a sense of God's wholeness, everything coming together for good, will come and settle you down.

'It's wonderful what happens when Christ displaces worry at the center of your life.'

So, I suggest that worry is best dealt with by turning it into prayer and casting the underlying anxiety onto a heavenly Father who really does care for His children.

I started with *Fawlty Towers*. Let me finish with (as it were) *On the Buses*. A while ago, some atheists and humanists plastered Britain's buses with the slogan: 'There's probably no God. Now stop worrying and enjoy your life.' In my opinion, the very people who need to worry are those who really believe that there probably is no God.

❯ Mother Mary

KEY VERSE 'For He has looked upon the low station and *humiliation of His handmaiden*. For behold, from now on all generations [of all ages] will call me blessed and *declare me happy* and *to be envied!*' Luke 1:48 (Amplified Bible)

HOW DO WE picture God? Of course, it's impossible for our finite minds to comprehend His vastness. Some people see Him as just a very superior human. Others think of Him as so immense they cannot imagine Him at all. One thing must be true, though. For God to be God, He must possess all knowledge. He must contain the ability to know everything that was, that is and that will be.

Little nine-year-old Marie could not quite understand this and she asked her vicar the following question: 'God might know everything, but how does He know the good people from the bad people? Do you tell Him, or does He read about it in the newspapers?'

Now is not the moment to get into a debate on inherent versus total omniscience, and certainly not predestination. But both the Old and the New Testaments are full of verses that confirm that God has all knowledge. For example, in Psalm 147 the psalmist writes: 'God's understanding is beyond measure.' John in his Epistle tells us that 'God knows everything'. We worship a God who makes plans.

Being God, He must have known from the beginning that Man, His masterpiece, would rebel against Him. Being God, He must have known from the beginning that there would come a time when He would need to send His Son down to earth as humankind's Saviour. Being God, He must have known from the beginning of time what year, what day, what hour, what minute that would be. Being God, He also must have known from the beginning of time that a young teenage virgin called Mary would be the one to give birth to His Son.

In fact, according to the genealogy in Luke 3, God had already planned the family line, beginning with His first son, Adam. His plan for redemption was set, but He did not want it to be a secret plan. Over 700 years before that plan would be carried out, He broke the news to Isaiah: 'Therefore the LORD himself will give you a sign: the virgin will conceive and give birth to a son, and will call him Immanuel' (Isa. 7:14).

Then God gave another reminder, through another prophet: 'But you, Bethlehem Ephrathah, though you are small among the clans of Judah, out of you will come for me one who will be ruler over Israel' (Micah 5:2).

The years rolled on. And then at last the day of fulfilment came very close. Now, even the Christmas story does not really start with Mary and Joseph. We must remember that the custom of the day for the Jews was arranged marriages. It is very likely that while Mary was still a child, and Joseph (we presume) somewhat older, his father would have been on the lookout for a suitable wife for his son.

God, of course, must have planned that Joseph's father would at some stage meet up with Mary's father (sorry if this sounds a bit like the movie *Back to the Future*!). Presumably, Joseph's father appreciated what he saw in Mary's family and thought that in a few years' time little Mary would make an ideal wife for his son. The two fathers would then have made a contract together, which was called an engagement even though the engaged couple had usually never even seen each other.

A marriage in those days was far too serious a matter to depend on two people falling in love. When Mary reached her teenage years, she would have the option to back out, but of course in doing so would bring disgrace on her father and family. In fact, Mary must have agreed to marry Joseph and her engagement then became a betrothal. This was a binding contract for both her and Joseph and the only way out of it was divorce. The betrothal would have lasted a year and of course was a chance for the couple to get to know each other; but there would definitely have been no sexual relations during this time. At the end of the year came the wedding.

So, again we see God's amazing plan unfolding. At this point the story becomes very personal and we begin to see what an amazing person Mary was. Here she is, a young teenager who has honoured her father's wishes and is in her betrothal year, after agreeing to marry a man she hardly knows. That, of course, was nothing unusual in those days – but then comes the shocking part of God's plan.

Out of the blue the angel Gabriel appears and says: 'Don't be afraid, God thinks you're special. You will become pregnant and give birth to His Son.' Understandably, Mary is completely fazed by this revelation and her response is a very human one: 'How can this happen when I haven't had sex with anyone?' The angel explains that this will happen in a miraculous way.

At this point – as strange as it may seem – God's plan for the redemption of humankind waits momentarily on the consent of this young Jewish girl. Mary replies: 'I am the Lord's servant. May it be to me as you have said.' You can almost hear Gabriel breathe a sigh of relief. Mary's statement is not just a 'Yes, OK, if I must'. It is an 'Amen!' Joyful excitement! 'I'm ready. Let's go!' The angel leaves and it is all systems go for God's plan to be put into immediate effect.

But let's try and imagine what must be going through this young girl's mind even in her excitement. 'What will my parents think? What will Joseph's parents think? And what will Joseph, my husband-to-be, who I hardly know, think?' And then, of course, she remembers what the law in Deuteronomy says. If something goes wrong, she could end up getting stoned to death. Being a virgin, the physical side of things must also enter her mind. 'How will the Holy Spirit make me pregnant? What will I have to do?' Maybe even 'Will it be painful?' And of course there is no one on earth who can answer these questions for her.

Nine months later, what God had planned since the beginning of time is fulfilled in a humble stable. It's not surprising that all heaven goes crazy as the angels share with the shepherds the good news that Jesus has been born. They had been waiting a very long time for this to happen.

Please allow me now to share a personal word.

Being ordained and becoming part of the staff of a cathedral involved me in a massive learning curve. Before I became an Anglican, as you may know, I spent most of my time being a leader in various very free, very Pentecostal, very evangelical churches. One of the biggest challenges has been to get my head around the role of Mary. In my previous church, she was never referred to as 'the Queen of Heaven', or given any status other than as the obedient mother of Jesus.

Over the years, I have discussed this matter with some of my very Catholic clergy friends and they have been shocked to hear that other Christians cannot hail her as being 'full of grace' or even see her as 'the Gate of Heaven'. In my opinion, to say she was sinless or to raise her to a position only slightly inferior to the Holy Trinity actually detracts from the amazing person she was.

So far on my personal journey of discovery of the biblical Mary, I have come to the conclusion that she was a most amazing lady, who deserves to be honoured and respected far more than I used to honour and respect her. Maybe my little poem sums up my true feelings:

Mary, Mary, opinions vary
As to if you're Heaven's Queen.
Some say forever,
Some say never,
Some say you're in between.

Mary, Mary, opinions vary,
But the Bible's keen to record:
You're favoured and blessed,
Different from the rest,
You're the mother of Jesus our Lord.

❯ All together now

KEY VERSE 'I have a serious concern to bring up with you, my friends, using the authority of Jesus, our Master. I'll put it as urgently as I can: You must get along with each other. You must learn to be considerate of one another, cultivating a life in common.' 1 Corinthians 1:10 (The Message)

YOU PROBABLY KNOW I have been involved in Christian music for most of my adult life. In my early years, when I think I was slightly more controversial, I wrote and recorded a song with satirical lyrics to get a point across. At that time, you could use humour to put a message over in a sermon but not in a song, it seems. The chorus went:

'CofE Pente Bapt and Co Metha Congre Free Quake
    Put them together and what have we got? We got an umpti-uni-church break!'

Sadly, because of that song some Christian bookshops banned the album! But people had got the wrong idea. I was never against Christians from different denominations meeting together. In fact, most of my bookings at that time were with interdenominational groups such as Youth for Christ and Spring Harvest. What I was objecting to was the idea that one super-denomination or megachurch in which everyone ends up looking the same, acting the same and worshipping in the same way was God's plan. I praise God for different denominations and church gatherings because, although the foundations of our faith are the same, the way we express what we believe and worship varies. This is great because a new believer can find a local church that suits not only their theology but also their taste in music that might help to enhance their worship.

For years, I was a minister in the Pentecostal denomination, then for many more years I was a leader of a very free charismatic evangelical new church; and now I am one of the team at a cathedral. On a number of Sundays each year I still enjoy travelling and leading services in all different denominations ranging from the very high to the very informal churches. One service I so enjoy attending that now I invite myself to it twice a year is 'the Church in the Pub' (actually a club now, as the original pub shut down).

We start by eating bacon butties and chatting, then we sing our praises to God accompanied by a heavy rock band and then I preach. If I go on too long, the bar opens and I lose my congregation! The church's leader earns his living by being a professional Elvis impersonator. But don't knock it. They're getting a congregation of bikers and others, some of whom would never fit into any more 'normal' Sunday service.

I still love a freer modern style of worship, with a band belting it out; but I have also grown to love the liturgical, sacramental, choral/classical style of worship in the cathedral. The problem comes when people think that one is superior or (dare I say?) more spiritual than the other.

But Christian unity always seems to be a struggle. Maybe it would be easier if we all just remained in our own local churches where they do things just the way we like it (sometimes). That might please us, though, but I don't think it would please God. God has always seemed to like His people to be in unity even though He created them with different personalities.

In Old Testament times, He chose twelve sons of Jacob and so twelve tribes trudged around a wilderness for forty years giving Him and poor Moses major grief. After they crossed the Red Sea, there was a brand new start with a brand new leader called Joshua. It might have entered Joshua's mind to make a few changes for the sake of peace:

'OK, guys, to save the aggro, let's split up and have twelve different armies. Good luck to all of you and may the best army win!

'I'll stick with my mates from the tribe of Ephraim.'

But that could never happen. Why? Because no single tribe could be called 'the children of Israel'. God's plan was that all twelve were going to make up the Israelite army and march into the Promised Land. Each tribe was going to have to learn to live with and help the others. They had little idea of the troubles ahead but they were told not to fear but to stick close to each other and God. So, after a very long, very painful journey, they were going to move out into the new territory together. God wanted opposing armies to see that Israel's strength lay in trusting Him and supporting each other.

In the New Testament, Jesus chose twelve very different disciples. Again, with their different backgrounds and personalities we know there were tensions and arguments. After Jesus sent them out in twos, He could have kept that model. They could each have teamed up with someone they got on with. (I wonder who had the pleasure of pairing off with Judas?) But no, Jesus wanted them to keep their individuality but to stay as a team. It would always be 'the twelve apostles', not 'the six pairs of apostles'. He even told them that they should respect each other, stay humble and wash each other's feet!

So, today if God has made us collectively part of His family, how can we really call ourselves a family if we never want to meet up with our brothers and sisters of different denominations?

But there is another reason why we need to be together. No one church or denomination has all the truth, and certainly not all the gifts. In 1 Corinthians we read that Christ's Body is made up of many different members and if those members are not connected, the Body will not function properly. Many of us now believe that we need to work harder to bring about more unity, not necessarily by arranging more 'churches together' services but by more socialising, evangelising and serving our local communities interdenominationally. Although we may meet in different buildings, we want non-believers to see that we are a family who love and respect each other.

In Philippians 2:1–5, the apostle Paul writes:

'If you've gotten anything at all out of following Christ, if his love has made any difference in your life, if being in a community of the Spirit means anything to you, if you have a heart, if you *care* – then do me a favor: Agree with each other, love each other, be deep-spirited friends. Don't push your way to the front; don't sweet-talk your way to the top. Put yourself aside, and help others get ahead. Don't be obsessed with getting your own advantage. Forget yourselves long enough to lend a helping hand.

'Think of yourselves the way Christ Jesus thought of himself.' (*The Message*)

Thomas Manton, the 17th-century Puritan preacher, said: 'Divisions in the church always breed atheism in the world.'

So, I wonder whether, in contrast, unity in the church could bring about a new spiritual awakening and revival in the world. I think it's certainly worth a try, don't you? And we don't need to leave it to church leaders to get things moving!

Make mine a double!

'A pupil is not superior to his teacher, but everyone [when he is] completely trained (readjusted, restored, set to rights, and perfected) will be like his teacher.' Luke 6:40 (Amplified Bible)

ELIJAH WAS IN many ways a one-off. But, unlike some today who sadly seem intent on just building a ministry around themselves, he realised that as he got older he needed to find someone to hand the baton on to. This someone would have younger legs and a different personality, and might even be more mightily used by God than he had been! Of course, this would be no random selection, and certainly no CVs or interviews would be needed to find the successful candidate. God already had someone in mind and it helped that Elijah knew that bit of God's mind.

Reaching a field, he saw a farm worker called Elisha ploughing his land behind a couple of oxen. It must have been a strange experience for Elisha to see, out of the corner of his eye, an old man approaching him, walking across the freshly ploughed soil, negotiating the deep furrows nimbly. That would have been no problem for Elijah – he must have been one of the fittest guys in the Bible as he is recorded as being able to walk, and on the odd occasion even run, for miles over every sort of terrain.

As Elijah approached him, he didn't say anything. He just took off his cloak and threw it over Elisha's shoulders. I would imagine that Elisha was already hot and sweaty from his labours, so he must have guessed that this manoeuvre was not to keep him warm but was a symbolic call, which he gladly accepted. Of course, he may well have recognised Elijah on sight – the old man had made quite a reputation for himself!

The way Scripture talks about Elijah and Elisha, it's evident they had very different personalities. Elijah comes across as a stern, forceful and solitary person, while Elisha could definitely be firm if needed but was gentler, often choosing to be with others and showing care and concern for individuals.

In the middle of his half-ploughed field, Elisha knew at once that his farming career was over and, after saying his final farewells to his mum and dad, he was ready to follow his new master. Before they hit the road, though, he made a bonfire out of the plough and killed and cooked the oxen for dinner. He knew he wouldn't need them again. It was the end of an old life and the start of a new one.

For the next few years, Elisha served Elijah and treated him like a father figure. Soon, Elijah could see that his successor, being a fast learner, was fully trained and ready to succeed him. He knew that he had passed on all he could and, that being the case, his own ministry on earth was now completed. It was time for him to let Elisha take over and he knew he would not be around to get in his way.

Just a quick aside here. I have met quite a few older Christians in leadership who so-called 'hand over their ministries' to younger people but never actually get out of the way to give their successors the freedom to go on and develop something new and fresh. Older leaders can so easily become a cork in the bottle and stifle the next generation.

Back to our story. When they reached Gilgal, Elijah told Elisha to stay there, as the Lord was sending him a further eight miles to Bethel. There was no way Elisha was going to let his master out of his sight and so he replied: 'As surely as the Lord lives and you live, I will not leave you.' Close by there was a group of people known as 'the Company of Prophets' and they, too, told Elisha that Elijah would be leaving him that day. Elisha was already aware of that but did not want to hear about it.

When they reached Bethel, Elijah said to Elisha: 'Stay in Bethel. I'm going to walk a further twelve miles to Jericho.' Elisha's reply was the same as before: 'As surely as the Lord lives and you live, I will not leave you.' Again, the Company of Prophets told Elisha that Elijah was going very soon, and again he told them he was aware of that but did not want to hear about it.

When they reached Jericho, Elijah said to Elisha: 'Stay in Jericho, for the Lord is sending me a further six miles to the River Jordan.' By this time, you or I might be thinking, 'Is this guy trying to get rid of me?' Elisha knew better than that, however, and replied with the same words as before: 'As surely as the Lord lives and you live, I will not leave you.' He knew that if he wanted what Elijah had, he must go where Elijah went and do what Elijah did!

It was now that fifty of the Company of Prophets stayed in the distance. They seemed to be waiting for something unusual to happen. On reaching the river, Elijah rolled up his cloak and struck the water with it – and it divided. And both of them walked over on dry land. Elijah then turned to his successor and asked if there was anything he could do for him before he left him. I guess Elisha could have asked for anything, but there was only one thing he wanted from his mentor: a double portion of what he possessed spiritually.

For Elijah, this must have been a perfect reply, confirming that the right man to carry on his work was standing in front of him. All the same, he knew that only God could grant Elisha's request and that he couldn't make God's decision for Him, so he wisely said that if Elisha saw him go, that would be God's way of saying he would get what he'd asked for.

As they went on talking, a chariot of fire and two horses sent from heaven came between them. It was then that a whirlwind came towards them and took hold of Elijah and lifted him up away from the earth. Although Elisha knew it was time for Elijah to leave him, he was nonetheless distraught at his going and cried out after him, tearing his clothes at the loss of his mentor.

But he knew that this was God's plan and he also knew that as he had seen Elijah go with his own eyes, God must have granted him his request. He was, however, going to make doubly sure! Picking up Elijah's cloak, he walked back to the Jordan and, seeing the Company of Prophets standing on the far bank, he struck the water with it and shouted: 'Where now is the God of Elijah?' The waters parted and he walked across the river bed towards them.

The Company of Prophets knew at once that the spirit of Elijah was now in Elisha. Even so, against his wishes, they still insisted on going and looking for Elijah's body, just in case he had landed on a mountain or in a valley. Of course, they found nothing. Elijah had been taken up to heaven.

Elisha went on to prove that he had that double portion, as the Bible records that he was involved in twice the number of miracles Elijah had performed. Well, nearly. If someone had been following Elisha around counting miracles, they might have been just a little disappointed at the time of his death and burial, as he seemed to be exactly one miracle short of the required number.

But then we have that great story in 2 Kings 13:21. Some Israelites were burying a dead body when suddenly they saw a band of Moabite raiders. In terror, they threw the body into Elisha's tomb – and as soon as it touched Elisha's bones it came back to life and the dead man stood up! Perfect! That makes it exactly a double portion!

As you probably know, I've spent a lot of my life teaching many thousands of children about Jesus using contemporary music and methods. But while I was doing so I was also keen to help to train younger people, as I knew that, as the years went by, others would not only replace me but would also be more successful than I had been. I praise God that so many of the young people who were part of my team have gone on to be greatly used by God.

God has given you a specific ministry. I hope you are training up a successor or two!

〉I'm free

KEY VERSE

'Christ has set us free to live a free life. So take your stand! Never again let anyone put a harness of slavery on you.' Galatians 5:1 (The Message)

MY ONE AND only brush with the law happened when I was an arrogant eighteen-year-old. I was in court on a charge of dangerous driving and for some reason I started arguing with the magistrates, thinking I needed to explain the law to them before they could find me innocent. Not my best idea, and needless to say I was found guilty as charged and they threw the book at me. As well as a hefty fine, I was banned from driving. I fought the law and the law won. On reflection, rightly so!

In the Gospels, we often find Jesus fighting certain laws, and really giving the Pharisees a hard time. A few years ago, I wrote a little song for children that went:

'I don't want to be a Pharisee or anyone like that.
It's stupid swallowing camels, while straining out a gnat.
To keep the letter of the law, they forgot the people it was for.
I don't want to be a Pharisee or anyone like that!'

It was never destined to be a Wesley classic, of course, but it put a point over with which Jesus seemed to agree! ᖴ𝖠𝖱𝖡𝖫𝖤𝖣

Many Jews thought that Jesus had come to destroy the Law of Moses, but Matthew in his Gospel clearly states that this was never His purpose. The Law of Moses was only meant to be temporary. Jesus came as the fulfilment of Old Testament prophecy. The coming of the Messiah would bring these old laws of Moses to completion and herald the arrival of the age of grace.

But Jesus was not hammering the Pharisees for their observance of Moses' laws. No, they had taken things much further. The Pharisees had deliberately drawn up too many laws, knowing that Mr and Mrs Average had no hope of keeping them all. One day, a Pharisee invited Jesus to eat with him and was surprised that He didn't wash His hands before the meal.

Now, this was not a quick hand wash for cleanliness, this was a matter of ceremonial law. The law demanded that before a man ate, he must wash his hands in a certain way – and he must also wash them between courses. As was the norm with the Pharisees, they had planned every little detail.

Large stone vessels of water (like were used when Jesus turned the water into wine) were there specifically for this purpose. An exact amount of water had to be used. First, the water must be poured over the hands, beginning at the tips of the fingers and then running up to the wrist. Then, the palm of each hand must be cleansed by rubbing the fist of the other into it. Finally, water must again be poured over the hands, this time beginning at the wrist and running down to the fingertips. To the Pharisees, to omit the slightest detail of this routine was a sin.

Jesus was obviously very angry with them, for not only did He call them 'fools' but He followed that with half a dozen 'Woe to you!'s. Or, as *The Message* puts it: 'I've had it with you! You're hopeless, you Pharisees.' He was making the point loud and clear that if only they were as particular about getting their hearts clean as they were about washing their hands, they would be much better people!

Every denomination has religious traditions that are not particularly biblical. Now, of course there is nothing wrong with traditions – in fact, some can be quite helpful. The problem only comes when people try to force these traditions onto others and make anyone who disagrees feel like a miserable sinner.

So, what can we learn from the strong words Jesus said to the Pharisees? First, He does not want us to concentrate on externals. For the Pharisees, so long as the externals of religion were observed, that was all that mattered. But we are not on this earth to try to show people how spiritual we are by keeping church laws and traditions.

It's easy sometimes to impress people by showing outward signs of 'doing the Christian thing', but if we are lacking in love and justice, our lives are just a sham and a con. Man does look on the outward appearance, but it seems that God is far more interested in what is going on within our hearts. We may regularly go to church, read our Bibles and pray, be generous givers to good causes, and these are all very good things to do. But if we are not trying to love God with all our heart, soul, strength and mind *and* love our neighbour as ourselves, we are not living out the life of a true follower of Christ.

Secondly, Jesus does not want us to spend our lives worrying about details. Compared with love, kindness and generosity, the washing of hands and the giving of tithes with mathematical accuracy are unimportant details. How easy it is for us church people to get lost in totally unimportant details! I've heard people argue about how much water should be used for baptism, and whether we should use bread or wafers at the communion service. Some people seem to love arguing about the different styles of music used to encourage worship – they insist that some styles are right and others are just wrong. Jesus condemned the Pharisees for piling endless extra rules on ordinary Jews, making it impossible for them not to live in guilt.

Today, it's hard enough for us to live out the Christian life and do what Jesus asks of us without having people trying to impose more regulations and restrictions on us that go beyond the Bible. It is the Holy Spirit that draws us nearer to Jesus, not being bossed, controlled or forced to do and believe certain things by so-called religious people or denominations.

Let's conclude by joining in a real Wesley classic:

'My chains fell off, my heart was free,
I rose, went forth and followed Thee.'

Jesus gave His life to give us real freedom so we truly can follow Him. Of course, this freedom is not a freedom to do what *we* like, but a freedom to do what *He* likes.

Finally, as Paul says in Romans 6:14 (NIV): 'You are not under the law, but under grace.' This being the case, let's be thankful for the grace of God and enjoy our Christian lives and let's never allow any modern-day Pharisees to put chains back on us!

King Jealous who grates!

KEY VERSE

'The acts of the flesh are obvious:
... jealousy ...' Galatians 5:19–20

APPROXIMATELY 2,070 YEARS ago, there was a certain man who lived in Judea. This man made himself popular with the Romans, and Julius Caesar had such regard for him that he appointed him military governor. The man's wife gave birth to a son, who was half Jewish, and in his early thirties this son was declared 'King of the Jews' by the Roman Senate. He had his palace in the city of Jerusalem. He was no ordinary king. In fact, he was not even just a good king – no, he was a great king. Well, he thought he was, anyway.

No one can argue about the fact that he was a great builder. He oversaw the construction of the Temple as well as many palaces and fortresses. No one can argue about the fact that he was a great ruler. In fact, throughout his long (nearly forty-year) reign, he was the only ruler in Palestine to maintain peace. And no one can argue about the fact that he was very generous. History tells us that in times of need he helped the poor to pay their taxes to Rome. He even went so far as to melt down one of his own gold plates to buy corn for the starving. Yes, there can be no doubt about it: he was a great king. In fact, he was known as Herod the Great!

However, this great king, with all his great attributes, did have a great flaw in his character. He was insanely jealous that someone else might be as great as he was. Anyone he thought was getting anywhere near to being as great as he was, he had killed. This included his wife Mariamne, his mother-in-law Alexandra, his eldest son Antipator, and then he had his two other sons, Alexander and Aristobulas, killed. No wonder the popular saying of the day was 'It's safer to be one of Herod's pigs than one of his sons'!

Sometimes with age and maturity people see the error of their ways and change, but sadly this was not the case with Herod the Great. In fact, if anything he got worse. The older he grew, the more paranoid he became. Just before the birth of Jesus, he realised that he would not be around much longer but there were still a lot of very wise men in Jerusalem who were greatly respected and even loved by the people. Thinking that one of them could conceivably still upstage him, he had them all thrown in prison and issued the order that when he died they should all be executed. He hoped this might also mean that when people were mourning for these wise men, it would look as though they were mourning for him.

His legacy was thus secure. Herod sat back on his throne satisfied that he had no rivals left alive in his kingdom who could ever match his greatness. It was just at this point that some very intelligent men who studied the stars arrived in Jerusalem asking for the whereabouts of a newly born king of the Jews. They had come to pay Him homage, having followed a star for two years from the East.

Just a small aside. It's worth noting that just because these men brought three gifts with them doesn't mean there were actually three of them. There were probably quite a few people in their entourage, as they were carrying valuable goods and they would need protection from bandits on such a long journey.

Anyway, news of the arrival of these 'magi' (as they were known) looking for a new king reached Herod and, as you can imagine, it was the last thing he wanted to hear. He immediately summoned the priests and demanded information about this new king, this 'Christ child'. They explained that according to prophecy the baby would be born in a nearby town called Bethlehem. Herod secretly met the magi and found out when their star had first appeared. He then told them to go to Bethlehem and look for the child. Once they found Him, they must immediately report back to him so that he, too, could pay his respects.

Well, we all know the story from here. When the magi finally arrived in Bethlehem with their gifts, Jesus would already have been a toddler. And of course they never went back to inform Herod, having been told not to by an angel. As soon as they had gone, an angel advised Joseph that Jesus was not safe in Bethlehem because Herod was going to search for Him to kill Him. Joseph must take both the child and Mary to Egypt. He would be told when it was safe to return.

Just another little aside about God's provision. We know that Joseph and Mary were not well off because of what they did when the eight-day-old Jesus was consecrated to the Lord in the Temple. Rich people would offer a lamb as a burnt offering and a young pigeon as a sin offering; but that was expensive and so a special allowance in Leviticus said that anyone who couldn't afford a lamb could offer two pigeons instead. Which, of course, is what Joseph and Mary did. So, how on earth could this poor couple afford to travel to Egypt and seek refuge there? God's provision of gold, frankincense and myrrh arrived at just the right time!

Of course, Herod went mad when the magi failed to return, and what followed was the dreadful 'slaughter of the innocents'. He had calculated, from the timing of the appearance of the star the magi had told him about, that the new king must be under two years old. That's why he had all the boys up to the age of two who lived in the vicinity of Bethlehem killed. Herod the Great died a humiliating death. And, although without doubt he did some good things – in his early years, anyway – he will always be remembered for the wicked things he did.

When we talk about sin, jealousy is rarely mentioned as a major problem. I'd like to suggest that for some it can be. The dictionary definition of 'jealous' is when someone is suspicious or fearful of being replaced by a rival. We will always find people in our workplace, in our circle of friends and even, dare I say, in our church life who are better at doing things than we are. It's easy to become jealous of these people.

As we can see with Herod the Great, if jealousy is not confessed to God and dealt with, time does not make it go away but actually tends to make it worse. God made each of us special and unique. We really have no need to be jealous of anyone.

❭ Going up?

KEY VERSE *"'He'll wipe every tear from their eyes. Death is gone for good – tears gone, crying gone, pain gone – all the first order of things gone." The Enthroned continued, "Look! I'm making everything new."' Revelation 21:4–5 (The Message)*

AS A CHILD, I was not too keen on going to heaven. Having been brought up in a Christian community with strict rules, I thought that heaven would be an eternity of:

- not watching the television on Sundays
- wearing an uncomfortable suit plus a white shirt and tie ... and, to top it all
- I would have to spend every minute of every day singing long, dreary hymns or listening to long, boring sermons!

You may be relieved to hear that in my more mature years my thinking has changed! Our reading from Revelation informs me that heaven is a place where there will be no tears, no death, no mourning and no pain. I am looking forward now to going to heaven – but maybe not too soon! But perhaps I won't die. Maybe Jesus will return while I am still 'Deacon Ish'.

But will I be going up before Jesus comes down? In other words ... is there such an event as the Rapture – and if so, will it happen before Jesus returns?

What I am about to share may not be a major issue for some, but with my spiritual background I know that to other people eschatology, or end-times theology, is a very big thing. Although I have spent time studying the Bible, I am still unsure of the events that will lead up to the end. But there are some people who claim to know all the answers. For example, some believe in a literal Rapture, when only the believers are taken up from the earth to meet Jesus in the air.

The now infamous American preacher Harold Camping really was convinced this would occur on Saturday 21 May 2011 at 6.00pm. I believe Harold was still at his home in California on Sunday 22 May 2011, not where he thought he'd be – in the air with Jesus.

But even some atheists claim to take the Rapture seriously.

... entrepreneur from New Hampshire started a new business thanks to Harold Camping's prediction. He set up the Eternal Earth-Bound Pets website, which states the following:

'You've committed your life to Jesus. You know you're saved. But when the Rapture comes what's to become of your loving pets that are left behind? Eternal Earth-Bound Pets takes that burden off your mind. We are a group of dedicated animal lovers, and atheists. Each Eternal Earth-Bound Pet representative is a confirmed atheist, and as such will still be here on Earth after you've received your reward. Our network of animal activists is committed to step in when you step up to Jesus.'

Eternal Earth-Bound Pets attracted more than 250 clients who paid at least $135 to have their pets picked up and cared for after the Rapture.

'They will be disappointed twice,' the entrepreneur told the *Wall Street Journal*. 'Once because they weren't raptured and second because ... I don't do refunds.'

So, how is it all going to end? Please forgive the simplification! Many are convinced that the Rapture will come first, followed by a time of tribulation that all true believers will miss (the Tribulation, that is). Then the second coming of Christ will happen, followed by the thousand-year period (the Millennium) when the believers reign with Christ. Then, the final judgment and eternity. (This, of course, seems to imply that, if the Rapture counts as Christ's second coming, there will be a second second coming ...)

Others are convinced that we are in the Tribulation now and that the Rapture and the second coming will happen at the same time – and then will come the Millennium, final judgment and eternity. Still others are convinced that there will not be a Rapture at all!

Throughout history, the Millennium (Christ's thousand-year reign over His kingdom on earth) has been a very hot and divisive topic. It certainly was at my evangelical theological college. Throughout history, there has been serious conflict over millennial beliefs – indeed, some people have suffered and even died for them.

Ladies and gentlemen ... In the blue corner, we have Justin Martyr, Tertullian and Charles Spurgeon, who were reputedly staunch 'pre-millennialists'. They believed that Jesus' second coming would happen *before* His literal thousand-year reign on earth. And in the red corner we have Polycarp, Calvin and Luther, who were reputedly either post-millennialists (believing that the second coming will follow the Millennium) or amillennialists (not believing in a literal reign of Christ on earth at all).

With such heavyweight theologians battling it out with their own interpretations of Scripture, it again confirms to me that nobody but God really knows how it will all end. I myself – a simple Christian – am a staunch pan-millennialist. I believe it will all pan out all right in the end!

I question whether spending ages researching and debating end-time issues is making good use of our present time. Surely Jesus has far more important things for believers to do in their precious few years here on earth? It's hard to imagine Him saying in the Sermon on the Mount: 'Blessed are those who spend hours and hours researching how I am going to return.'

He does make one thing very clear, though, which many people seem to ignore.

He tells us in Mark 13:32, 'About that day or hour no one knows, not even the angels in heaven, nor the Son, but only the Father.' Perhaps the end times are supposed to remain a mystery, understood only by God Himself.

However, the Bible does assure us that the Lord's return will not be secret or silent. Matthew's Gospel declares that everyone will see Him 'coming in the clouds'. We shall see the angels; we shall hear the trumpet blast – accompanied, 1 Thessalonians tells us, by a mighty shout from an archangel. No one knows the date when Jesus will return, but everyone will certainly know when it is happening.

Perhaps, instead of being so concerned about when and how the end will come about, believers would be wiser to follow the wisdom of Peter and Jesus. In 2 Peter 3:9–14, Peter urges believers to be repentant, holy, godly, zealous and at peace, waiting for the Lord's coming with eager expectation and joy. Jesus simply said: 'Be prepared and keep watch.'

However God chooses to close this age, Jesus promises that there will be a heaven awaiting His followers, where He reigns and where there will be no more tears, death, mourning or pain. Although there will always be much we don't know, we can be sure of this:

'Great is the mystery of faith.
Christ has died.
Christ is risen.
Christ will come again.'

Hallelujah! Hallelujah!

David's trouble and strife ... s!

KEY VERSE 'Honor marriage, and guard the sacredness of sexual intimacy between wife and husband. God draws a firm line against casual and illicit sex.' Hebrews 13:4 (The Message)

IN ANCIENT GREECE, women used to reckon their age from the day they got married rather than the day they were born. It was thought that a woman's life only began once she was married. Later on, in England, a man could divorce his wife in Anglo-Saxon times on the grounds that she was too passionate. And, coming even more up to date, in the Victorian era women librarians were told never to place books by male and female authors next to each other unless they were married.

Time to look at a mighty king, a mighty warrior but not quite such a mighty husband. After he beat Goliath, David's promised reward was to marry King Saul's eldest daughter, Merab. However, just before the wedding Saul married her off to someone else.

But all was not lost. Saul's second daughter, Michal, was madly in love with David. It appears she was rather a strange lady and Saul seemed pleased to offload her onto David, maybe thinking she would be a right pain to him. The dowry Saul demanded was neither gold nor precious stones. All he wanted from David was a hundred Philistine foreskins. Very romantic! David, always willing to go the extra mile it seems, brought him 200. He married the woman he had literally fought for, but soon after he discovered that his father-in-law wanted to kill him. So, he abandoned Michal and went on the run. At this point, he married again. This time it was to Ahinoam, who gave birth to his first recorded son, Amnon.

While still an outlaw, with an army behind him, David met Nabel, a rich idiot of a man, and his beautiful and intelligent wife, Abigail. David sent some of his men to ask Nabel (whom he had been protecting) for food. Nabel told them to get lost. So, David mustered his troops and headed towards Nabel to make sure that *he* got lost. But the intelligent Abigail intervened.

She brought David a lot of food and drink and told him her husband was a wicked fool. David accepted her apology.

When she got back home, she found Nabel partying and drunk. The following morning, when she told her husband what she had done, it seems the news was too much for him to cope with and he had a heart attack! Ten days later, he died. David then married Abigail. Meanwhile, back at the palace, Saul had married David's first wife, Michal, off to someone else. Are you keeping up?

After Saul's death, David wanted Michal back and so he dragged her away from her new husband, who was obviously very much in love with her. By now, David had also married Maacah, who gave birth to a son called Absalom and a daughter called Tamar. Both happened to be very good-looking. At some stage he married Haggith, who gave him another son, called Adonijah. David then captured Jerusalem and took more wives and concubines and had many more children.

You probably know the story of the return of the Ark of the Covenant to Jerusalem, when David danced with all his might wearing only a linen ephod (which was a priest's upper garment). Michal was watching and found his lack of clothes embarrassingly revealing. She was furious at him for being so vulgar in front of slave girls – but David said that he did it for the Lord and would become even more undignified still! Or, as the Bible puts it:

'Michal, Saul's daughter, came out to greet him: "How wonderfully the king has distinguished himself today – exposing himself to the eyes of the servants' maids like some burlesque street dancer!" David replied to Michal, "In GOD's presence I'll dance all I want! He chose me over your father and the rest of our family and made me prince over GOD's people, over Israel. Oh yes, I'll dance to GOD's glory – more recklessly even than this. And as far as I'm concerned … I'll gladly look like a fool … but among these maids you're so worried about, I'll be honoured no end."

'Michal, Saul's daughter, was barren the rest of her life.' 2 Samuel 6:20–23 (*The Message*)

And finally, Bathsheba. Again, a well-known and tragic story. David saw, stole and made pregnant the wife of one of his most loyal soldiers, Uriah – and then had him killed on the battlefield. After David married Bathsheba, she gave birth to their son; but God was very angry with David for what he had done and the child became ill and died. Bathsheba's second son, though, was special. He was to be David's heir and his name was Solomon. He was one of the wisest men that ever lived – but maybe not that wise, because he had 700 wives and 300 concubines. By disobeying God's law in Deuteronomy 17, his heart was turned away from God by the influence of the women he married.

So, did having many wives work for David? Like many other men in the Old Testament, he loved some of his wives, was sexually attracted to others – and some, it seems, just brought him grief!

At this point, we need to ask the question: What did God think about His friend David – and many others in the Old Testament – marrying so many women? Tricky one, this. Many Christians, including Martin Luther, have argued that polygamy is acceptable. It's hard to find anything in the Bible that condemns it outright, although Matthew 19:3–9 is the key text in terms of arguing for monogamy. There must be a reason why God permitted and overlooked polygamy, even though we can see with Adam and Eve that His original intention seems to have been one man one woman.

In Old Testament times, there seem to have been far fewer men alive than women. We know, too, that their numbers decreased dramatically with every war. It was the men who went out to battle, and usually the men who got killed in their thousands. Then, we must remember that we are talking about a patriarchal society. It was nearly impossible for an unmarried woman to provide for herself. Many women were uneducated and unskilled and their main function was to look after the home and produce children. They would have depended on fathers, brothers and husbands for protection and provision. They had to survive somehow in a world short of men.

And God certainly did not want His chosen ones marrying men from other nations. In those days, a husband's responsibility was to look after all his wives and concubines. Just maybe God overlooked polygamy at this time so that many women who otherwise, with so few men around, would have no hope of finding a husband could still find protection and provision. Well, that's one answer – even if it may not be the right one!

Just a few nice quotes on love and marriage to conclude:

'The perfect marriage begins when each partner believes they got better than they deserve.'

'A successful marriage requires falling in love many times, always with the same person.'

And finally:

'Don't marry a person you can live with, marry somebody you can't live without.'

For me personally, having one wife is enough. For my wife, Irene, I'm sure that having one husband is more than enough!

❭ It's a wonderful life!

KEY VERSE

'Anyone who loves his life loses it, but anyone who hates his life in this world will keep it to life eternal. [Whoever has no love for, no concern for, no regard for his life here on earth, but despises it, preserves his life forever and ever.]' John 12:25 (Amplified Bible)

A WEALTHY BUSINESSMAN was shocked to see a fisherman sitting beside his boat, playing with a small child. So, the businessman asked: 'Why aren't you out fishing?'

The fisherman replied: 'Because I've caught enough fish for one day.'

'Why don't you catch some more?' the businessman enquired.

'What would I do with them?' said the fisherman.

'You could earn more money,' the businessman explained. 'Then, with that extra money, you could buy a bigger boat, go out into deeper waters and catch more fish.

'Then you would make enough money to buy nylon nets. With them, you could catch even more fish and make even more money. And then with that money you could own two boats, maybe three. Eventually, you could have a whole fleet of boats and be rich like me.'

'And then what would I do?' enquired the fisherman.

'Why, then you could really enjoy life,' said the businessman.

The fisherman looked puzzled and asked: 'What do you think I'm doing now?'

But *should* either of them be enjoying life? Once a year, I celebrate a rather strange anniversary. On 10 April 2008, I was lying in a hospital bed in Chichester having just been diagnosed with acute myeloid leukaemia. Although I knew my survival was in God's hands, not mine, rightly or wrongly I felt that I could either fight this cancer and hope to live a few more years or give up and take an early one, to be with Jesus. There were many reasons why I wanted to live a little longer. My family, my friends and my ministry were just a few of them. So, I fought to live.

Life and death are a bit of a paradox for the Christian. Of course we are looking forward to dying because that means we will be with Jesus; but we also quite enjoy life down here! I really do love life in this world – not all the time obviously, but for the vast majority of it – and I am forever praising God that I have been granted a bit of extra time on earth. But am I wrong to be enjoying life?

Judging by our Bible verse from John's Gospel, it looks on first reading as though I could be, but what did Jesus really mean when He said those words? Let's consider His own life. Were His thirty-three years on earth so miserable He just wished He could be transported back to heaven ASAP?

I believe that, for much of His life, the sinless Jesus felt the same ups and downs that we feel. Of course there were times He would have disliked, maybe even hated. He would not have enjoyed encountering people who were hostile to Him and didn't disguise the fact that they didn't like either Him or what He said. He would have felt sad when people like the rich young ruler lacked faith. He clearly felt grief when He was at Lazarus' grave, and immense distress when He was contemplating the fate of Jerusalem.

During what we now call 'Holy Week', we are reminded of some of the times Jesus probably least enjoyed. He had to cope with one of His closest friends betraying Him, another denying Him and all of them deserting Him. He had to face false accusation, humiliation, mockery, physical and mental torture and then, on the cross, extreme loneliness.

Good enough reasons for Jesus to hate this life on earth? Well, yes and no, because that is only half the story. From a lot of the details we can glean from the Gospels, there was much in life that Jesus seemed to love. He enjoyed walking and talking with the twelve apostles. He enjoyed eating and drinking and going out for meals with friends. He enjoyed the company of little children. He enjoyed spending time with the outcasts, misfits and so-called sinners whom other religious people rejected. He enjoyed seeing tormented individuals being released from demons, and the sick, suffering and disabled being healed and restored.

He got excited when people like the centurion showed faith. He was overjoyed when the seventy disciples He sent out returned to Him with wonderful stories. And even with the horrors He endured on the road to Calvary, He knew that only through this suffering could the world know forgiveness and have a chance to be made right with God.

I am so relieved that Jesus did enjoy much of His life on earth. It means that He also wants us to enjoy our lives. So, what does that verse really mean?

John Wesley wrote in his notes: 'He that loveth his life – More than the will of God; shall lose it eternally: and he that hateth his life – In comparison of the will of God, shall preserve it.'

Jesus seems to be suggesting that if our love of life is built only around selfish pleasure and ambition and we choose to leave Him out of our lives, our future once we leave this world looks pretty bleak – to put it mildly. He wants us to put Him first in our lives. He wants to share in both the good times and the trials we face while on earth.

Jesus never taught that the life of the believer would be one hundred per cent enjoyment. To take up our cross daily and follow Him means we are expected to expose ourselves to danger, persecution and sacrifice. He wants us at times to step out in faith and trust Him and (dare I say it?) even take some risks occasionally.

Of course, some Christians may think they will live longer if they hide away, trying to avoid all 'spiritual battles', and just sit in front of the television with their slippers on watching the God Channel. Well, there is a chance they may live a little longer down here, but they will never experience that exciting life that Jesus promises to those whose desire is to do God's will.

Finally, a word about the picture Jesus gave of the grain of wheat. Only by death comes life. A single grain of wheat is little use. But once it is thrown onto the cold ground and buried there as if in a tomb, it will bear fruit. Jesus, like a grain of wheat, had to die and be buried if there was ever to be an everlasting harvest. And we, too, are involved in this harvest; but first we, too, need to die to 'living for ourselves' and be reborn and start 'living for Jesus'.

Poor hyper-intelligent Nicodemus! It's easy to see why this very learned man couldn't get his head around the idea that he needed to be 'born again'. Jesus said: 'Nicodemus, to be my follower you need to die as far as your old life is concerned and experience a rebirth. The impossible needs to happen. The old will go and all things will become new.' Although nowadays some people abuse the term 'born-again Christian' by applying it to an exclusive members' club for evangelicals, I believe that every true believer has been reborn into a new life. For some, this happened instantly; for others, it may have been a prolonged process. 1 Peter 1:3 says: 'Praise be to the God and Father of our Lord Jesus Christ! In his great mercy he has given us new birth into a living hope through the resurrection of Jesus Christ from the dead.'

Jesus says: 'Whoever serves Me must follow Me.' So, it seems that in serving Jesus and putting Him first in our lives not only will we find true enjoyment in life down here but we can also look forward to even more enjoyment with Jesus in heaven. As Ezra Taft Benson put it: 'When we put God first, all other things fall into their proper place or drop out of our lives.'

❯ Being a loyal supporter

KEY VERSE 'This is the assigned moment for him [Jesus] to move into the center, while I slip off to the sidelines.' John 3:30 (The Message)

FOR THE PAST forty years, I have felt that my calling as a travelling evangelist, both home and away, has been to try and 'shake up' the lost and 'wake up' the found!

By the mid 1960s, pop music had well and truly taken off. Every Thursday night in Worthing Assembly Hall, famous chart groups would appear. Sometimes, they travelled straight down from London after an appearance on *Top of the Pops*. Jimi Hendrix, Cream, The Who, to name but a few, would regularly perform there. Usually, an unknown support act was put on first to help fill up the evening – and at the age of sixteen I was a singer/guitarist in one such outfit. You might need a good imagination to believe it now, but the band I played in was called the Hansom Beasts.

It was a terrible gig. While most of the audience stayed in the bar, the few who ventured into the main auditorium amused themselves by yelling obscenities at us and throwing various missiles at the stage. Some even threw coins. We were not very good, admittedly, but what made us sound even worse was when halfway through a song our bassist stopped playing and started picking up the money and pocketing it. Of course, no one ever came to see the support act – everyone was desperate to see the headliners. I knew the deal.

The disciples likewise knew the deal when they were walking around with Jesus. Their role would always be a supporting one. There was no way they could or ever would distract attention from the main star.

The fourth Gospel was written to present Christianity in a way that Greeks would understand, so it's not surprising that it's only in John that we read about some Greeks coming to find Jesus. Now, the Greeks may have had some strange characteristics, but they did have a reputation for being thinkers and seekers after truth. The particular men mentioned in John 12 were probably God-fearing Gentiles who had come to Jerusalem for the feast of Passover.

They approach Philip (maybe because 'Philip' is a Greek name) and greet him with great respect: 'Sir, we wish to see Jesus.' They don't mean that they just want to *see* Jesus – they probably can already see Him. And they aren't just interested in Him because He is a celebrity. No, they want to meet Him – in other words, to get to know Him and discover what He is all about.

Philip, whom John sort of puts down throughout his Gospel as a bit slow and indecisive, is unsure what to do. So, he goes to get advice from Andrew. Andrew knows exactly what to do, and takes the Greeks to Jesus. He knows that Jesus will never refuse to see anyone who genuinely seeks Him. Here we have one of the first faint hints of a gospel that will eventually go out to all the world. When the Greeks approach Jesus, there is no reference to Him saying to Andrew and Philip, 'Brilliant! Bring them over here, I'd like to meet them.' Jesus appears to ignore them. But He doesn't. Their arrival has told Him that something major has taken place. Jesus has repeatedly said that one day the 'hour of glory' will come, and now, as He looks at these Greeks who, He knows, represent a waiting Gentile world, He realises that that hour has indeed now come. This is the sign that the time has come to lay down His life.

Jesus goes on talking about seeds and plants, life and death and servants and masters. But He struggles with the thought of what is to come and is thrown into momentary turmoil. He knows He will soon be entering the enemy's territory, to drive the ruler of this world out of his domain. He knows that soon that prince will be dethroned and a new King will draw both Jew and Gentile to Himself. He also knows that, to bring this about, He must first suffer disappointment, heartbreak and, ultimately, an agonising death. So, He lets the Greeks know that if they really want to find out the reason He is on this earth, they need to stay around for a short while and watch as He completes the work His Father has sent Him to do. He finishes by saying: 'And I, when I am lifted up from the earth, will draw all people to myself.' In a short while, all will be drawn to Jesus by the world-conquering power of love He displays as He hangs and dies upon a cross.

As I've said, Philip and Andrew and all the disciples knew they would always be playing a supporting role to Jesus. But it was an important role they were playing. The Greeks sought out Philip but only so that ultimately they could see Jesus.

I guess there are two people in Jesus' life whom some might say deserve star billing. First, there is Mary. Unique. The mother of God's Son. The

Magnificat reminds us that 'all generations shall call [her] blessed'. She was a very special lady, but she always knew she was in a supporting role to Jesus and at one point even said, 'Whatever He tells you to do, do it'. Then there is John the Baptist. Jesus Himself said there was never anyone born greater than John, but John himself knew his supporting role and told everyone: 'Jesus must increase and I must decrease.'

Did God need people to play supporting roles? Well, the obvious answer is no. God, being God, does not need anything or anybody. Yet throughout history He has always had people here on earth who have played supporting roles. And, today, we are all still playing a supporting role to Jesus.

Some people go into a church just to experience the choir. That's great, but if they leave only praising the music they will have somehow missed the point. The singers and musicians are playing a supporting role to Jesus and our prayer is that people will leave praising Him. Some people go into a church just to listen to a powerful preacher. That's great, but if they leave happy just to have heard an eloquent sermon they will have missed the point. The preacher is playing a supporting role to Jesus and our prayer is that they will hear His voice. Some people go into a church just to find friendly people. That's great, but if they leave having only met friendly people, they will have missed the point.

Some people come into Chichester Cathedral just to admire the windows, the paintings and the nine-century history. That's great, but if they leave having just seen a historic old building they will have missed the point. Even the building is playing a supporting role to Jesus and our prayer is that people will feel His presence there. Our prayer is that they will feel the love of Jesus in God's people and, even more important, realise the love Jesus has for them.

All of creation exists to play a supporting role. Our purpose in life is to point other people to our Saviour, the Lord Jesus Christ, who was lifted up high upon a cross. And, as we do this, Jesus will draw all people to Himself.

Forgive me, Father. I feel guilty.

KEY VERSE

'I remind you, my dear children: Your sins are forgiven in Jesus' name.' 1 John 2:12 (The Message)

AS A SONGWRITER, I know that certain songs I write can become very precious to me. However, I have found that there are some odd people around who seem to love to desecrate serious songs. Their corruption of the lyrics can sometimes be quite clever and amusing, but it rarely makes us songwriters laugh.

Many years ago, I wrote a song called 'Father God, I Wonder'. The chorus includes the words 'I will sing your praises'. Surely no one could mess about with those lyrics? Oh yes they could! I arrived at one church expecting to hear 'I will sing your praises' but instead I heard one joker singing, 'I will ping your braces'. And of course everyone thought it was hilarious – except me! Fortunately, it never caught on – as very few of the younger generation even know what braces are!

On a visit to Walsingham, the Anglo-Catholic centre otherwise known as the Anglican Shrine of Our Lady of Walsingham, I had to smile when I heard the congregation singing, 'Shrine, Mary's shrine' instead of 'Shine, Jesus, shine'. I'm not sure my buddy Graham realised when he wrote that hymn that with some slight word changes it could be enjoyed by such diverse extremes in the Christian community!

But the worst corruption of a song I have heard was to one you may remember written by a friend of mine called Mick Ray in 1978, titled: 'I get so excited, Lord, every time I realise'. It was great until someone changed the words at the end of the first line from 'I'm forgiven' to 'I'm a gibbon'. Strangely, many youth groups have enjoyed singing the latter version far more than the original – and added insult to injury by jumping around like apes while they sang it! It's a shame because they have missed the wonderful truth of the song. Personally, I really do get excited when I realise that the Lord forgives me.

Once a year in the cathedral we celebrate All Saints' Day. So, who and what is a saint – and is a saint still a sinner who needs to be forgiven? The word 'saint' is derived from the Latin word *sanctus*, which simply means 'holy one'. Anyone who is referred to as a saint has been recognised as having an exceptional degree of holiness. Most recognised 'saints' performed miracles and many died for their faith as martyrs, but none came to be regarded as saints because they were so holy they were perfect! They were all sinners and all needed forgiveness just as we do.

Nowadays, many church services have a similar format. It begins with musical praise and worship, followed by a sermon. The sermon often concludes on an emotional note with a challenge. This, of course, can be Holy Spirit-inspired, but it can also amount to manipulation by the preacher. Often at this point some of the congregation feel guilty and feel the need to repent, confess and receive prayer.

The worry is when the preacher emphasises that 'you' need to do this or that. Not 'we'. As a preacher myself, I find it's quite easy when faced with an audience of sinners to forget that I am one myself. I know, too, that it's far easier to make people feel guilty than to let them feel forgiven.

Often, you can go into a service like this feeling pretty good but by the time the preacher has finished making you aware of your shortcomings, you can feel pretty lousy! And sadly that is sometimes even after prayer. Jesus loved sinners but not their sin. From the tone and the words used by some preachers, I get the impression they don't love the sin *or* the sinner.

Having come from a very different background, one thing that attracted me to the cathedral Eucharist was the format of the service. We begin with a prayer of confession and absolution. How can we truly worship until we have done that? But, unlike many churches, the sermon is never the climax of the service. We always end on what should be a wonderful high by sharing in the bread and the wine and having communion with Jesus before being sent back out into the world to share His love with others. So, we may start the service feeling lousy sinners but there is no reason why at the end we shouldn't all leave feeling forgiven and close to Jesus.

There are two very important things to say about forgiveness, though. The first is, Jesus taught in Matthew 6 that we must forgive others: 'For if you forgive other people when they sin against you, your heavenly Father will also forgive you. But if you do not forgive others their sins, your Father will not forgive your sins' (Matthew 6:14–15).

Of course, I'm not saying that this is an easy thing to do. We have all hurt others and everyone I know has been hurt by others, and sadly those others are often fellow Christians. Some have been so hurt that forgiveness seems impossible – but I believe that Jesus can help to make it possible.

One of the most amazing examples of forgiveness occurred in 2005. Eighteen-year-old Anthony Walker was killed with a mountain axe by two thugs just because he was black. His mother drew on her Christian faith to find forgiveness for her son's murderers. When asked outside court if she forgave them, she said: 'Do I forgive them? At the point of death, Jesus said: "I forgive them because they don't know what they are doing." I've got to forgive them. I still forgive them. My family and I still stand by what we believe: forgiveness.' A wonderful example to all of us!

So, we need to forgive others – but we also need to accept that, whatever we have done in the past, Jesus loves and forgives those who confess. 'If we confess our sins, he is faithful and just and will forgive us our sins and purify us from all unrighteousness' (1 John 1:9). Of course, nothing can change amazing grace and the love God has for us. The author Philip Yancey correctly says: 'There is nothing we can do to make God love us more. There is nothing we can do to make God love us less.'

But we still need to accept and receive that love and forgiveness for them to mean anything. Living in guilt and not accepting that Jesus has forgiven us makes us very sad people. There is no way we can enjoy living the 'life to the full' that Jesus promised His followers unless we believe and accept this.

So, all sinners can become all saints – and saints know what it is to rejoice in the wonderful forgiveness Jesus has provided. As Adrian Plass writes: 'The shameful wonderful fact is that we can be forgiven. Shameful … because we are reminded again and again that the righteousness is not ours, and there are times when we Christians hate to be reminded of that. And wonderful … because it is a free and willing forgiveness from a Fatherly God that will bring us safely home one day.'

Let's conclude by endorsing Mick Ray's original words: 'I get so excited, Lord, every time I realise I'm forgiven!'

Could Jairus cope?

KEY VERSE

'Don't overlook the obvious here, friends. With God, one day is as good as a thousand years, a thousand years as a day. God isn't late with his promise as some measure lateness.' 2 Peter 3:8 (The Message)

WHILE ON EARTH, Jesus communicated His message in various ways. Sometimes He preached, sometimes He taught but often He just told His listeners stories. Nowadays, it's the stories and parables we most often use to teach children, but Jesus often told stories to His most intelligent listeners to get His message across. Throughout this book you will notice a bit of preaching, a bit of teaching and quite a bit of storytelling. One thing I love doing is retelling stories from the Bible.

Jairus was ambitious. I believe that from an early age he had made it a goal in life to one day become the president or leader of his local synagogue. Why do I think that? Well, it was a position usually held by a layman, which meant he would not get paid for doing it and so he would have to carry on doing his day job at the same time. This was never going to be a career prospect for Jairus, but more of a vocation he must have deeply desired. A synagogue leader would be required to do a lot of hard work and would have needed a fair amount of training as well as a good education. It was a job that had great spiritual responsibility and demanded respect.

The Greek word *synagoge* means simply 'a place of meeting'. At the time when Jesus was on earth, there were around 480 synagogues in Jerusalem alone. The synagogue was a social centre where Jewish people could gather together each week to meet each other. It was also a place where adults could be reminded of the teaching of the Law and children could be given instruction in the ancestral faith. A synagogue leader would probably be elected by the local elders. As well as overseeing the five-part service each Sabbath, which included prayers, psalm singing, blessings, reading from the Scriptures and teaching on the sacred passages, he was the president of the board of elders, responsible for the good management of the synagogue and one of the most respected men in the community.

Jairus must have been really pleased when eventually his dream came true. But how often disaster strikes just as everything seems to be falling into place! That certainly was the case for him. Having achieved his life's ambition, he was faced with a serious family problem. His twelve-year-old daughter became very ill. It goes without saying that, being a loving father, he would have consulted all the best doctors of the day, but each one gave the same tragic prognosis: 'Your daughter is going to die.'

Now, Jairus must have heard that Jesus had a reputation for healing people miraculously, but he would also have been aware that He had been branded a lawbreaker and had already been banned from several synagogues. For him to seek out Jesus would mean putting at risk the synagogue leadership he loved so much. However, his little girl was far more important to him than anything else – and this man Jesus was Jairus' last hope. The Bible tells us that he sought Jesus out and when he eventually found Him he fell down before Him, pleading with Him to come to his house and heal his daughter.

Jesus must have recognised Jairus and would have realised what it was costing him to make this request. He agreed to go with him. However, Jairus wanted Jesus to come quickly and yet He didn't seem to have the same sense of urgency – and the large crowd that surrounded them only made the journey slower. Now, a woman in the crowd had been suffering from internal bleeding for twelve years. (I'm sure it's no coincidence that she had been suffering for as many years as Jairus' daughter had been alive.) This woman believed that if she just touched Jesus' clothes she would be healed. She pushed through the crowd and reached out her hand and touched His cloak – and immediately knew that she had been made whole. Jesus sensed that power had gone out of Him and He stopped and asked who had touched Him. The disciples said it could have been anyone – the crowd was pushing them all over the place!

At this point, let's try and put ourselves in Jairus' shoes. 'What's the big deal, Jesus? Someone *may* have touched you, but surely I'm your priority. Someone else may have jumped the queue for your attention, but time is running out for my little girl while you're trying to find out who it was.'

The woman came forward and owned up. She explained her situation and Jesus was impressed by how much faith she had. Again, the anxious Jairus could have been forgiven for wondering why Jesus was wasting time conversing with this woman when, unlike his little girl, she was not on the critical list and, let's face it, she had already lived many years. Jairus' young daughter had not. Why on earth was Jesus wasting so much time?! Then it happened. Someone from Jairus' house arrived to tell him it was too late, his daughter had died. In other words, no need to bother with Jesus now – He had been too slow.

Imagine poor Jairus! Total confusion. If only Jesus had walked more quickly! Jesus must have seen the confusion, the sadness and despair in the face of this loving father – and He told him not to worry, just believe! Then came His promise: She *will* be healed. This would have been a good time for Jairus to hear the words of our reading: 'God isn't late with his promise as some measure lateness.'

Outside his home it was chaos. Professional mourners had arrived and were causing mass hysteria, working on everyone's emotions by weeping, wailing and playing doleful tunes on flutes. These people were actually paid to do this. Jesus told them to be quiet as the little girl was not dead, just sleeping. The mourners must have thought: 'What does He know? We've seen the girl, He hasn't. We know she is dead!' They switched from grieving to mocking, laughing at Jesus and making fun of Him.

Jesus went inside the house with Jairus, Mrs. Jairus, Peter, James and John, and they all saw the little girl lying in front of them, drained of life. With no colour in her cheeks, no pulse and no breath, to everyone but Jesus she did not look as though she was just sleeping! Jesus held her hand and said in Aramaic: *Talitha koum*! Which means: Little girl, get up! And then the miracle took place. Her heart began to beat again. She started breathing and the colour came back to her face.

Most of the New Testament is written in Greek, and the two other accounts of this story, in Matthew and Luke, leave out those two little Aramaic words that Jesus spoke over the dead girl. But, as we know, Mark's Gospel is really Peter's Gospel, and many years later as Peter himself recounts this story to John Mark, he can't help recalling Jesus' command in the very words He used: *Talitha koum*. For him, I suspect, they were synonymous with the little girl coming back to life, in what was probably one of the most amazing miracles he ever saw Jesus perform.

Finally, Jesus told the girl's parents to give her something to eat. It seems a strange thing to say, really. Surely, if He could bring her back from the dead He could bring her back with a full belly! Maybe He wanted to show that she was fully alive and not just a ghost or an animated corpse. Or just maybe, like most children, this little girl had a favourite food and Jesus wanted her mum and dad to go and prepare her a special celebration treat.

If we really had been in Jairus' shoes, I think that most of us, on being told that the girl had died, would have thought it was too late for even Jesus to do anything. At times, we may feel that God is not fulfilling His promises as quickly as we would like Him to, especially when we face difficult times in our lives. Maybe even, like Jairus, we may be questioning whether it is too late for even Jesus to do anything about our situation.

We must keep faith and believe that with God it is never too late. He will always fulfil His promises – but in His time, not ours.

❯ Deep purple

KEY VERSE

'He wants not only us but everyone *saved, you know,
everyone to get to know the truth* we've *learned: that there's*
one God and only one, and one Priest-Mediator between
God and us – Jesus, who offered himself in exchange for
everyone held captive by sin, to set them all free. Eventually
the news is going to get out.' 1 Timothy 2:4 (The Message)

IN MY SUNDAY school days, we would often sing the chorus of a hymn written by James Slack in the late nineteenth century, which understandably was a favourite of the Salvation Army. The chorus went:

> 'Steadily forward march! to Jesus we will bring
> Sinners of every kind, and He will take them in.
> Rich and poor as well, it does not matter who,
> Bring them in with all their sin;
> He'll wash them white as snow.'

Although Mr Slack was a little too slack in my opinion and probably deserves to have his poetic licence endorsed for attempting to rhyme 'who' with 'snow', the song does have some good biblical content. Jesus is ready to take in and forgive sinners of every kind, whether rich or poor. If we take a look at Acts 16, we can see how true this is.

But let's begin at the beginning. Up to this point, the Holy Spirit has prevented Paul entering the Roman province of Asia, but then one night he has a vision of a man begging him to go to Macedonia. Paul is convinced that at last God is giving him the green light and so he sets off. First stop is Philippi, a city founded by Alexander the Great and now a Roman colony. The place was full of people who were proud to be Roman citizens. Many of them were retired soldiers who were still very loyal to Roman culture and Roman law. People knew Philippi as a 'Rome away from Rome'.

It seems there were so few Jews in the city that there wasn't even a synagogue – and it only took ten Jewish householders to form a synagogue!

So, on the Sabbath Paul and his friends decide to pray by the River Gangites. Here they meet some women who worship God but are not followers of Jesus, so Paul and his friends sit down and begin to share the good news with them. It's worth remembering here that in his vision Paul had seen a man, not a woman. How he has changed! The old Saul of Tarsus would have known the rabbinical saying, 'It is better that the words of the Law be burned than be delivered to a woman!' But we don't find Paul searching for a man now. Obviously, that was no longer his way of thinking!

One of the women was called Lydia. She was a 'God-fearer', a Gentile who openly worshipped with the Jewish women. We know she was a very wealthy woman at the top end of the social scale, who came from Thyatira, a city about 100 miles north of Ephesus. She traded in purple cloth, and the dye used (which had to be gathered from a particular shellfish drop by drop) was very expensive. The Bible tells us that the Lord opened her heart and she responded to Paul's message and both she and the other members of her household were baptised.

She then has a challenge for Paul. She tells him that if he really does accept her as a believer in the Lord, he can prove it by coming to stay at her house! I think she must have been quite a persuasive lady, as Paul seldom stayed with his converts but on this occasion he takes up her offer. Lydia's household was the first in Europe known to have been converted to Christianity and baptised.

But as so often happens when something good comes about, something annoying follows. From now on, every time Paul and his friends (probably Luke and Silas) leave Lydia's house to go to their prayer meeting, a fortune-telling slave girl follows them shouting: 'These men are servants of the most high God who proclaim to you the way of salvation.'

Now, these words sound correct and if any Jews had been around they would have assumed she was speaking of the one true God of Israel. But there were no Jews around, only pagans. And to any pagans who heard her, her words meant something very different. Remember that they worshipped various 'most high' gods, so to them the girl might have been referring to Zeus or Isis or even some Roman god. They would have taken the term 'most high god' to refer to whichever deity they personally considered to be supreme.

Anyway, Paul doesn't see this as a good starting-point for a debate. Day after day, it is just confusing everyone. He also knows that it is an evil spirit speaking, and it's wearing him out. He doesn't want even a hint of the gospel or the name of God to be promoted by demons. So, using the all-powerful name of Jesus, he casts out the evil spirit that possesses the slave. Unfortunately, she has been earning a great deal of money for her owners by telling fortunes and now they are furious because her 'gift' has gone. So, Paul and Silas are dragged before the magistrates and end up being flogged and thrown into prison.

It's interesting to note that they are locked in the inner cell with their feet fastened in stocks. I'm guessing the authorities must have thought that if these guys have the power to cast out spirits, who knows what other powers they might be able to use to break out of prison!

Well, Paul and Silas start praying and singing hymns so that all the other prisoners can hear them whether they want to or not! Maybe all the prisoners do want nothing more than a good sing-song, but hey! It's the middle of the night and I dare say a few are shouting at Paul and Silas to shut up as they're trying to get some sleep!

Then comes an earthquake, which opens the doors of all the cells, and everyone's chains fall off! The jailor is about to kill himself, as he assumes that all the prisoners have escaped, but Paul stops him and tells him they're all still there. The jailor falls down before Paul asking what he must do to be saved.

'Believe in the Lord Jesus', says Paul, 'and you will be saved, you and your household.'

The jailor washes their wounds and then he and his household are baptised. He then feeds them, filled with joy because he and his whole family have come to believe in God. Paul and Silas are released that day and return to Lydia's house, where they encourage their converts and no doubt tell them that the jailor and his family will be joining the newly formed little church of Philippi.

It was to this little Christian community in Philippi based on the house of Lydia that Paul later wrote, from another prison cell, a letter full of happiness, gratitude, affection and reassurance. Lydia was certainly a key person in the foundation of the Christian church in Philippi. So, Jesus was ready to accept the rich – the upper-class Lydia. He was ready to release the poor – the possessed and abused slave girl. And He was ready to save the life of the working-class jailor.

Praise God that forgiveness, release and salvation are available to everyone!

Gone fishing

KEY VERSE *'Is there anyplace I can go to avoid your Spirit? to be out of your sight?' Psalm 139:7 (The Message)*

A FEW YEARS ago, Irene and I took a break in Lanzarote. As we were relaxing in the bar, a man and his wife walked in. The man was looking very upset. Irene whispered that I should talk to him, but I must confess that my initial thought was, 'Why? After all, I *am* on holiday'. But after a further nudge I quickly remembered that there is no such thing as being on holiday from being a Christian. The man explained that he had just heard that his mother had died. I offered to visit him in their apartment the following day to pray for him and, although he was not a churchgoer, he readily agreed.

When I turned up the next day, I found him sitting on their balcony, posed for prayer, but his wife was standing nearby armed with a video camera. She explained that they wanted her to film me praying so that friends at home could watch it later. It was one of the hardest prayers I have ever prayed. I wasn't sure whether I should look at the bereaved man, close my eyes or smile at the camera. But God has promised that He will always be with us, wherever we are and whatever we are doing. And that seems to include holidays!

Peter discovered something similar while he was taking a rather odd short break. He had two obvious accomplishments: he was good at fishing (since that was the way he earned his living) and, as we discover later, he was a strong, influential leader. Right from the earliest days of his relationship with Jesus, he knew the deal. Jesus had said to him and his brother: 'Come, follow me and I will make you fishers of men. Your expertise may lie in catching fish, but I am going to transform it into something far more beneficial.' Of course, at the time Peter would have had no idea what Jesus was talking about!

However, he immediately left his boat and his nets and, as far as we can tell from Scripture, put his fishing career very much on the back burner so that Jesus could begin to train him to be an evangelist. So, for the next three years none other than the Son of God Himself trained Peter. During that time, he saw impossible healings and other miracles, including dead people coming back to life.

He saw Moses (who had been dead for 1,300 years) and Elijah, who had disappeared in a whirlwind nine centuries earlier. At the same time, he saw Jesus transfigured. He was close by when Jesus was accused, tortured and then crucified. He was probably one of the first people to see Jesus after He rose again from the dead. He'd had Jesus breathe the Holy Spirit into him and had been given a commission to go and make disciples. And now, with all the heavens waiting expectantly for a whole new era called 'Christianity' to begin, we read in John 21 ... he's decided to take a bit of a break and take up fishing again. What makes it even more interesting is that more than six other disciples – some of whom may not even have been fishermen – followed his example and decided to have a night out with him!

Why? Surely there was something far more important they should have been doing? Some have suggested that Peter and some of the others wanted to give up! They'd tried the disciple thing and decided to go back to the good old days with their boats and nets on Galilee. Life was far less complicated and dangerous messing about on a lake.

Others have suggested that they were hard up! After all, they weren't earning any money. Maybe they needed to get some fish to make a bit of cash, or even just to provide the supper for the night. Personally, I think they were just plain fed up! Just sitting around, maybe even waiting for Jesus to reappear, was boring, so Peter took the initiative and said: 'I'm off fishing. Does anyone want to join me?' But God had promised that He would always be with them, wherever they were and whatever they were doing. And that included taking a night off and having fun fishing.

However, since Peter had met Jesus his fishing skills seem to have disappeared. The Gospels do not record a single instance when he manages to catch even one fish without Jesus' help, and this occasion is no exception. Maybe the words Jesus spoke in John 15:5 are coming home to roost: 'Apart from Me you can do nothing.' After a long night with no luck, a stranger on the shore tells them to cast their net on the other side of the boat. It's as they are pulling in a miraculous catch that they realise the stranger is Jesus.

Peter decides to jump overboard to go and meet Jesus and leaves the other guys to bring in the bumper haul. Jesus doesn't seem annoyed or disappointed with any of them. In fact, the opposite – He addresses them as friends. There is no hint that He would have preferred them to have stayed at home and had a night of prayer or a Bible study rather than going out and doing something they seem to have enjoyed.

Recently, I have changed my way of thinking. I believe that God does have specific plans for us while we are on earth, and tasks He wants us to undertake, but I no longer believe that He has quite the rigid, minute-by-minute celestial daily planner for each of us that some people think. I think He expects us to use our brains, to take initiative and make decisions, and (unless He gives us specific guidance) I don't think He particularly minds where we choose to go or what we choose to do. So long as we stay close to Him, there will always be things He can teach us and people to whom we can show His love.

Up until my illness, I felt that the main place where I could serve God was on a stage or in a pulpit, facing a large crowd. But lately I have discovered that sitting by a hospital bed or chatting to someone in a pub has been just as effective a way of serving God and showing the love of Jesus to people. Or even talking with people as I go around a golf course – although, being competitive, I find it harder sometimes in that context to consistently demonstrate His love!

Here, Peter is discovering the same thing. What probably started out as a fishing trip to break the monotony ends up reminding him that he needs God's help 24/7 – and that, wherever he is, God is there, too, with something to teach him. Finally, after breakfast on the beach, we overhear one of the most intimate conversations recorded in Scripture. Jesus says to Peter: 'Do you love me more than these?'

The obvious assumption is that He is pointing to all the other men sitting around them, but He may also be indicating the fishing boat and the gear. 'Peter, are you willing to make everything secondary to Me? In the past, you have trusted in your fishing skills for survival. From now on, are you willing to trust that I will supply all your needs?' Three times Jesus asks Peter if he loves Him – probably in answer to the three times Peter has denied his friendship with Him just a short while earlier. Jesus then informs him that as well as being a fisherman he is about to become a shepherd. Although the book of Acts does not record that Peter went on any more fishing trips, it wouldn't surprise me if he did when he felt like a short break.

So, to sum up, whether we are working, resting or playing, God is with us and has things for us to do, things for us to learn and His love to share with others. All we have to do is try and stay close to God and not allow other things to come before Him.

And to pray the prayer:

'Send us out in the power of Your Spirit to live and work to Your praise and glory. Amen.'

Making a healthy prophet

'Don't you dare lay a hand on my anointed, don't hurt a hair on the heads of my prophets.' Psalm 105:15 (The Message)

What about Agabus?

WE FIND THIRTY people who are specifically called a 'prophet' or 'prophetess' in the Bible, but only four are named in the New Testament: John the Baptist, Barnabas, the John who wrote Revelation and Jesus, whom we will look at later. Some prophets were called on by God to write down their prophecies, some were called to speak them and some were called to act them out. God often used drama to get people's attention, and some prophets went to extreme lengths to get their message across.

We find Isaiah being told to go barefoot and naked for three years. Yes, Isaiah was the original streaker! He certainly used an unconventional method to get people's attention. The message was graphic and clear: Repent or be stripped naked like Isaiah! Then Jeremiah was told to wear a yoke on his neck to emphasise God's message that King Zedekiah should submit to Nebuchadnezzar.

Ezekiel was called on to act many times. On one occasion, the Lord told him to pack all his bags and carry them around Jerusalem in the sight of the people as a sign that if they didn't repent, God would send them into exile. Another time, God told Ezekiel to lie down on the ground on his left side for 390 days, one day for each year of Israel's iniquity. When he'd finished that ordeal, God told him to turn over and lie on his right side for forty days, for the forty years of Judah's iniquity.

The Lord even ordered Ezekiel to play in a sandpit! He had to label a brick 'Jerusalem' and build little ramps around it to illustrate the siege of the city that was to come if the people didn't repent. Ezekiel's hardest acting assignment came when the Lord revealed that the prophet's wife would soon die. God instructed him not to mourn for her but to go on with what he was doing as if nothing had happened. When people came and asked him why he wasn't mourning, he had to say that if they didn't repent they would be overcome by a conqueror so swiftly that they would not even have time to weep.

In my opinion, though, the greatest prophetic actor of all must be Hosea. The Lord told him to find a woman of loose morals and marry her. It must have been one of the hardest things God ever asked a righteous man to do! Hosea obeyed, and God told him to explain the meaning of his action. The message was that Israel was like that woman when God selected them as His Chosen People. They were not picked for their beauty or wisdom or righteousness. They had no merit. They were selected by grace.

This was insulting for the Jews. They didn't understand what being 'chosen' meant. They thought they were better than other people, and in their spiritual arrogance they refused to listen to God's prophets when they called for repentance. When Hosea returned home from his preaching tour, he discovered that his wife had not been faithful and was having an affair with someone else.

Hosea's heart was broken. God told him to explain the meaning of her action. The message was that, like Hosea's wife, Israel had been unfaithful to God and had chased after foreign gods. And, like Hosea, God's heart was broken. When God spoke to him again, He asked him to do something incredible. He told him to swallow all his pride and to go and love his adulterous wife and buy her back again. She didn't deserve it. She had not repented. But Hosea obeyed. He paid the price, and she was redeemed. In this way, God used a prophet to act out the story of what He would do for us at the cross when He paid the price of His Son to redeem us from our unfaithfulness.

Prophets usually confirmed their calling by dying as martyrs, their lives taken from them. Isaiah is said to have died under King Manasseh by being sawn in two. Jeremiah is said to have been stoned to death by his own people in Egypt. John the Baptist's head ended up as the prize demanded by a young dancer, courtesy of a drunken king.

The book of Deuteronomy gives two basic practical principles that can be used to identify a false prophet. The first is that if they speak in the name of, and deliver messages from, another god or gods, they are automatically condemned for apostasy. The second is that if they make a prediction and it doesn't come true in due course, they are judged to be false. In both cases, they have to be put to death.

In the Old Testament, the prophets were largely passing on a message proclaiming 'the day of the Lord' and future salvation. Most of it was fulfilled in Jesus and linked in with His proclamation of the kingdom. The prophets helped people to see a different future: that whatever problems they were facing, things could be different.

But what about prophets in New Testament times and today? Of course, the most important prophet was Jesus. We get the idea that He was a prophet from two sources. The first is the people who identified Jesus as a prophet but not as God. And the second is Jesus Himself. He referred to Himself as a prophet when He was in Nazareth (Mark 6:4) and also said that Jerusalem was a killer of prophets (Matt. 23:37), which seems to anticipate His own death there.

So, what is the definition of a prophet? Well, a prophet is a person sent by God. They don't choose their task, they are chosen for it. All but Jesus recognise their inadequacy for their mission but for them there is no escaping it. A prophet is God's mouthpiece: they don't give their own opinions.

A prophet is a person through whom God speaks – often giving news people don't want to hear. A prophet takes instructions from no one but God and is answerable to no one but Him. A prophet brings people God's commands. Not good advice, open to debate, but commands. Prophets speaks out against sin – their function is to turn people back to God. Also, generally prophets were preachers and told parables, and many were born to be martyred. Prophets are always ready to lay down their lives for truth and to seal their message with the seal of their own blood.

Now we can see why Jesus was a prophet. He came from God. He used prophetic methods – parables and symbols – to get His message across. He was the supreme servant of God. He brought us God's commands, not just good ideas. It was His main aim to turn people from their sins back to God. He laid down His life to seal His message. Although 'Prophet' is one of Christ's titles, it is not the whole story. Believing in Jesus just as a prophet will not save anyone.

Although Jesus was in many ways the fulfilment of the prophets' work, Paul tells us to encourage each other to prophecy. We still need to pass on God's messages to others in order to strengthen, encourage and comfort them. However, when someone prophesies today, Paul tells us, they must never lose control and others need to weigh up what they say and confirm that it is from God. A prophecy is not just someone tacking on 'God says' before making a statement. And how do we know today whether it's a genuine word from God? It's exactly the same as in Old and New Testament times: the prophecy will come true without any manipulation from humans.

Today, many people may 'prophesy' but there are few 'biblical' prophets, because (as we have seen) true prophets have to live up to their own message, will put their calling before home and family and are willing even to die to get their message across.

All you need is love

KEY VERSE

'Love your enemies. Let them bring out the best in you, not the worst. When someone gives you a hard time, respond with the energies of prayer for that person.' Luke 6:27–28 (The Message)

THINGS WERE NOT going very well for the King of Syria. He was at war with Israel and, although he was probably very good at planning battles, he didn't seem to be able to win any of them! The King of Israel at this time was Joram, who was not a king who pleased God very often. However, there was a prophet living in Israel who did please God and his name was Elisha. And it seems that at this point Joram and Elisha were quite close.

The main problem the poor old King of Syria had was that every time he got his officers together to work out a plan of attack, the army of Israel seemed to find out what it was. It happened time and time again. The King of Syria was understandably furious and suspected that there must be a spy in his camp. It was time to assemble all his officers and flush out the traitor.

One of his officers had the courage to speak up. He explained to His Majesty that none of them were spies. He had heard that it was someone called Elisha who informed the King of Israel about all their movements. He'd even heard that this Elisha seemed to know about everything His Majesty did – even what went on in his bedroom!

The King of Syria had had enough of both his strategy and his privacy being invaded. He ordered his men to find out where Elisha lived and he would send an army to seize him. They duly discovered that Elisha lived in Dothan, which was about ten miles north of Joram's capital city of Samaria, in a very strategic location with good views of the roads going north-south and east-west. The King of Syria assembled a large force of cavalry and chariots and sent them by night to Dothan. This might seem a little extreme when they were only after one man, but obviously the king considered that this Elisha, who knew everything about him, was going to be a tricky person to capture! While it was still dark, the Syrians surrounded Dothan. It was Elisha's servant who first went outside the house and, to his horror, found himself confronted by a large military force who all seemed to be staring in his direction!

In a panic, he ducked back inside the house, found his master, told him the situation they were in and asked him what on earth they were going to do. Now, although the Bible doesn't say so, I can imagine a slight smile creeping over Elisha's face. Here was a man with not an ounce of fear, who was totally confident because he could see something his servant couldn't. He told him to calm down because those who were with them far outnumbered those who were outside in the Syrian army.

At this point, you can imagine the servant doing a quick bit of mental arithmetic. 'Well, there's my master and me, that makes two; and then there's me and my master, and that still adds up to just two of us. How can he say what he's saying? I know there are far more than two people in the army outside!' Elisha saw the confusion his servant was in, so he asked God to open his spiritual eyes. It was only then that this man saw that the surrounding hills were full of horses and chariots of fire! Funny, for some reason a movie theme tune and the name 'Vangelis' have just sprung to mind …

As the Syrian army closed in, Elisha prayed an odd prayer: he asked God to blind them. Only one other time in the Bible does someone make such a request and that is when Paul is faced with the evil sorcerer Elymas. On every other occasion, the prayers are that blind people should be able to see. God answered Elisha's prayer and as he approached the Syrians he found them in chaos, not knowing which direction to go in. Elisha spoke to them and told them they were at the wrong city and if they followed him, he would lead them to the right one.

Now, you need to try and picture this. An army of sightless soldiers on horses and chariots being led ten miles by Elisha, who was probably walking! Joram would have seen this strange sight approaching long before they reached Samaria. The city gates would have opened and Elisha would have led the Syrians through them. Once inside the city walls, Elisha asked God to open their eyes again and they would have seen they were trapped, surrounded by the army of Israel. Of course, Joram would have been very excited – it was like Christmas come early for him! Eagerly he asked Elisha: 'Should I kill them, Father?'

'Certainly not!' replied Elisha. 'This situation is nothing to do with you. Give them some food and drink and let's party! We'll make friends with them, and then we can send them home again.'

So, a great feast was prepared and these enemies became friends. After that, there was no war between these two countries for a long time. God wants us to make friends, not enemies!

Talking of which, a strange thing happened to me a while ago. I had popped into my local pub with my iPad and was sitting quietly in a corner looking at it with earphones on. After a while, a guy approached me, looking furious. He was very aggressive and in very colourful language he ordered me to switch my iPad off. He said that a pub is a place to talk, not look at those things. He was not just angry, he was almost out of control! I knew I had three options.

Obviously, I couldn't hit him – that wasn't really the Christian thing to do. But I could:

- ignore him and leave the pub quietly;
- tell the management (whom I know well) and get him thrown out;
- try to make friends with him.

I felt that the third was the right thing to do, so I packed my iPad away and went and stood next to him and his mate at the bar. I apologised if I'd upset him, but he just told me straight to bleep off! I told him I was not going anywhere; he had said that a pub was a place to talk, so I was going to stay there next to him and talk to him. He told me again in no uncertain terms that he didn't want to bleeping talk to me and to bleep off again! I went nowhere and even offered to shake his hand and buy him a drink. With many more bleeps, he flatly refused both offers.

Well, to cut a long story short, this banter (and bleeping) went on for quite a while, but I knew that God was up to something. Gradually, this guy started to calm down, and by the time I had to go we had had a really good (and revealing) conversation. I left having made a new friend, whom I have chatted to many times since!

Why am I telling you this? Well, I discovered that it's easy to react to or else ignore those who hate us, curse us or mistreat us for no reason at all. It's a lot harder to try and win them over and make friends with them as (it would seem from our Bible verse) Jesus wants us to. I'm glad I stuck with it – though, as my daughter commented afterwards, I was lucky he didn't smack me one!

Weeping and gnashing!

KEY VERSE

'Don't quit. Don't cave in. It is all well worth it in the end. It is not success you are after in such times but survival. Be survivors! Before you've run out of options, the Son of Man will have arrived.' Matthew 10:22 (The Message)

I WAS BORN in Bristol and as a very little boy I was very close to my gran. She often came to stay with us and, whenever she did, I would creep into her bedroom as soon as I woke up and talk to her. But there was a mystery. Why could I never decipher a single word she was saying first thing in the morning, and yet once she was up and dressed, her speech became crystal clear? One day, the puzzle was solved. That morning as I went in to my gran, I saw on her bedside table a glass jar and in that jar were two rows of teeth smiling at me.

Later, when I was growing up in a Christian community, I will never forget one hellfire preacher who was expounding Luke 13:28. As was expected from such a preacher, he emphasised the 'weeping and gnashing of teeth' and then added: '… and if you have no teeth, they will be provided!' My vivid imagination immediately went back to my gran's bedside. Not only was there going to be a line of the doomed awaiting damnation, there would also be millions of jars of false teeth so that even the toothless could join in the gnashing!

These are just the memories of a young boy. I don't wish for a moment to trivialise the serious warning Jesus gives in Luke 13. Jesus is making His final journey to Jerusalem when someone asks the question: 'Lord, are only a few people going to be saved?' Or, to put it another way, would many people enter the kingdom of God? The questioner probably thinks he knows the answer already. He and all the other good Jews will be saved, but the bad Jews and all the Gentiles won't be joining the chosen few in heaven.

On reflection, maybe he is really asking the wrong question. How many will be saved is not really the issue. The big question he should perhaps be asking is: 'Lord, will I be saved?' Of course, corporate worship is important and so is being a member of Christ's Body, the Church; but, as we know, the

Church is made up of individuals and Romans 14:12 reminds us that each of us will be accountable to God. It's our personal relationship with God that is the crucial thing on which we should all be keeping an eye.

Jesus gives rather a shocking answer. Entry to the heavenly kingdom is never automatic and is always the result and reward of striving. The word for 'striving' is the word from which we get the word 'agony', so Jesus is promising that the narrow way will not be easy. He goes on. The heavenly kingdom is like a house with a narrow door offering limited admission. Once the feast begins, the door is shut and no one outside will be allowed in to join the party.

There will still be those standing outside who feel sure they deserve to get in. 'Lord, you must remember me!' they will say. 'I've been one of your guests before. We've eaten and drunk together and we're good friends.' But it will be no use anyone trying to claim friendship with Jesus if they have never responded to His message. Others will say: 'Lord, you remember me! I was in the crowd when you were teaching, and not only that, I'm also well acquainted with Jewish doctrine and law.' But it seems there will be no automatic admission for Jews or for anyone else who claims to be 'religious'.

Then come some of the most tragic words in Scripture. Jesus will say to these people: 'I do not know you.' He will not only disown them but will discard them, with the words, 'Away from Me!' Then, accusing them of being evildoers, He will tell them they were just acting their religion, standing in His presence and yet actually doing the work of the devil. Heavy stuff.

The questioner will have found this answer hard to deal with. Jesus is saying that some Jews will be excluded while some Gentiles will be admitted. Then comes the punishment for those who are not saved. In Scripture, salvation and judgment cannot be separated from each other. *agreed*

On my travels, I meet many people whom I believe (without meaning to sound in any way judgmental) live a rather precarious spiritual life. Some think that just being part of our Christian civilisation means that all will be well for them in the future. But living in a Christian civilisation does not make someone a Christian, just as sitting in the choir stalls does not make someone a good singer. Others think that once they have made a commitment to Jesus or been 'born again', they have done all God requires of them. By making that one decision, they have 'bought their ticket to heaven' and are sure of their final destination. They feel that they can continue just to do their own thing in the blessed assurance that, because 'Jesus is mine', heaven's narrow door must surely open up when they arrive at it.

As I say, in my opinion both of these seem rather precarious ways of living. I believe there is no finality in the Christian life. We keep striving to go forward until the very end, or else we slip back. The summit of the mountain we are climbing will never be reached in this world. For the Christian, both the young and the not so young, life must always be upward and onward.

I believe that the heavenly kingdom will be full of surprises. I think that everyone will be amazed at both the enormous number and the variety of people who end up inside the doors of the salvation party. I am encouraged by 1 Timothy 2:3–4, which says that 'God our Saviour … wants all people to be saved'. Not just a chosen few, or even a mere 144,000.

My job as an evangelist is to keep reminding both myself and others that it is not enough just to hear the words of Jesus – we need to keep acting on them. It's not going to be enough just to sing 'What a friend we have in Jesus!' Jesus requires His friends to prove that they love Him by making every effort to be obedient to Him.

In about 1869 the Rev John Ernest Bode wrote the words to what was to prove a very popular hymn:

'O Jesus, I have promised
To serve Thee to the end …'

I find those words hard to sing. If I could rewrite them, I would change them to:

O Jesus, I'll try my hardest
But it's only through Thy grace and mercy that I will manage to serve Thee
to the end …

I appreciate that the new wording might be slightly difficult to fit to the tune!

One final thought. Our time on earth is a preparation for eternity. Let's keep on serving others and giving generously to those in need, because although our motivation should never be personal gain or reward, the Bible teaches that God does take note of our acts of love and kindness towards others. The proud in this world will be made very humble in the next, while those who nobody seems to notice will be made princes.

And a last little story. There was a Christian woman who had everything she needed and more. She had pampered herself with every luxury and expected everyone to serve her. She lived in a world built around herself and gave little to others. When she died and arrived in heaven, an angel was sent to conduct her to her celestial dwelling. As they walked past many fantastic mansions, she kept asking: 'Is that one mine? Is that one mine?' 'No,' the angel kept replying. As they reached the outskirts of the heavenly city, the houses became a lot smaller until finally, on the very edge of things, they came to a small wooden shed. 'That is your house,' said the conducting angel. 'What?!' said the woman. 'I can't live in that!' 'I'm sorry,' said the angel, 'but that's all we could build with the materials you sent up while you were on earth.'

Jo goes against the flow

KEY VERSE 'Point your kids in the right direction – when they're old they won't be lost.' Proverbs 22:6 (The Message)

ABOUT 2,600 YEARS ago, a baby boy named Josiah was born in the palace in Jerusalem. He had a bit of a tragic start to life because, when he was just five years old, his grandfather Manasseh, who was the reigning king, died. However, he had been a wicked king who turned the nation's heart away from God. The successor to the throne was Josiah's father, Amon. Sadly, he, too, proved to be a wicked king and when Josiah reached the age of seven he witnessed his father's assassination in his own house at the hands of his own servants. The Bible names Josiah's mother as Jedidah. It seems reasonable to assume that she and others encouraged her son to believe in the one true God and to do the right thing.

Josiah was crowned king at the tender age of eight. We hear little more about him until he reached his mid teens, but we do know that he didn't follow in his grandfather and father's footsteps and do evil. In fact, at the age of sixteen he became really serious about following the God of King David and renounced the corrupt belief in more than one god that had been encouraged by many of the kings who went before him.

At this time, Josiah's views may have been listened to by only a few and may have affected only those fairly close to him; but the good news is that a spiritual reformation had begun. It was about this time that Assurbanipal, the last great king of the powerful but rapidly waning Assyrian Empire, died. This would explain how a sixteen-year-old king could defy Assyria's insistence that Judah should honour its gods, which of course his grandfather and father had been happy to do. At the age of twenty, Josiah's radical reform spread throughout Jerusalem and beyond. It was around this time that Jeremiah started prophesying, which would have been an encouragement to him. But things really began to change when he reached the age of twenty-six.

Josiah could see that God's Temple was in ruins and so he instructed the high priest to collect money from the people as they came to worship, which was given to the building superintendents so that they could hire masons and carpenters and start the repair work. He never asked for any receipts because he regarded the superintendents as honest men. While the Temple was being repaired, Hilkiah, the high priest, discovered a scroll. This may have been Genesis to Deuteronomy, or maybe just Deuteronomy.

Before Josiah, there had been a long line of kings of Judah – in fact, fifteen in total. Of these, only five had been good and two mostly good. Two had been mostly bad and six totally wicked, the worst being Josiah's father and grandfather. That is why all record of God's laws had been lost and not even missed. Josiah listened as the rediscovered scroll was read to him, and he tore his robe in anguish when he realised how far Judah had fallen away from God. He knew that God must be angry with them and he asked his godly friends what they should do.

In charge of the palace tailors' shop was a prophetess called Huldah and she prophesied as follows: God said He was going to destroy Jerusalem because the people had forgotten Him and worshipped other gods. God's anger could not be assuaged but, because Josiah had humbled himself, wept and torn his clothes in shame and guilt, the destruction would happen only after his death.

Josiah assembled all the leading people in Judah in the Temple and read them the entire book of God's laws, and they all promised to obey God. Theory sorted. Then came the practical action. Anything in the Temple to do with Baal, Asherah and the sun, moon and star gods was taken out and burned. The homes of the male shrine prostitutes were destroyed and the corrupt priests and temple guards were put to death. Everything that was connected with heathen worship or idolatry was smashed or slaughtered and the mediums and spiritists were expelled. Josiah also reintroduced the Passover celebration.

Sadly, despite all his reforms, he never really succeeded in changing the hearts of the people. After his death, his son Jehoahaz succeeded him and, even though his own reign lasted only three months, managed to turn the nation back to the wicked ways of Josiah's father and grandfather. Josiah was the last godly king to reign over Judah.

It's also very sad because it seems almost as if Josiah's death was unnecessary. History tells us that Necho II, the King of Egypt, was advancing through Palestine to attack the Babylonians and Josiah led his army out to intercept him. Necho sent messengers to Josiah telling him that he had no argument with him and Josiah should stay out of it. He even underlined the point by claiming that God had told him to hurry and if Josiah insisted on blocking his way he would be opposing God and would be destroyed. Josiah refused to back off and went into battle. Even though he was in disguise, he was shot and killed by Egyptian archers. It seems tragic that Judah's godliest king met his end at the age of only thirty-nine because he didn't listen.

An exciting story of a great king, but let's finish near to where we began. What an amazing woman Josiah's mother, Jedidah, must have been! Her husband was a wicked man who had done all he could to turn the nation away from God. She was surrounded by false gods and powerful people who were a bad influence and yet she brought her son up to believe in the ways of the one true God. It just goes to show how important a part even one parent can play in bringing up their child in God's ways.

Looking back on my own childhood, I can see how being brought up in a Christian community and being influenced by not just my parents but also some very spiritual 'uncles' and 'aunties' have made a great impression on my life and helped me throughout my many years of ministry. Of course, however hard parents try to bring their children up in God's ways they cannot blame themselves if at an older age a child chooses to rebel and go in a different direction. There is no way I can blame either my parents or other Christians around me that in my teenage years I rebelled against all they had taught me and lived a very non-Christian life. It was my choice and, although they prayed for me, they had to allow me to live my own life and learn by my own mistakes.

So, parents and fellow members of the Body of Christ … Let's not just leave the training up of children to Sunday-school teachers and children's workers. We all have a part to play. We all must take responsibility to be a godly influence and share with younger children – by both word and example! – what the Bible teaches us about the Christian life.

❯ Golden oldies!

KEY VERSE

'I will cry to God Most High, Who performs on my behalf and rewards me [Who brings to pass His purposes for me and surely completes them]!' Psalm 57:2 (Amplified Bible)

AT THE BEGINNING of Luke, we read about a very godly priest called Zechariah and his wife, Elizabeth, who lived in the Judean hill country. (Only the chief priests lived in Jerusalem itself.) This couple were childless and far too old now to have children. More than likely, they were well over 60. This made Zechariah's personal life a tragedy. According to rabbinical tradition, seven sorts of people were excommunicated from God and one of the seven was a Jew who had a wife but no children. Childlessness was valid grounds for divorce in those days.

In the Bible, it always seems to be the woman's fault if there are no children and so we are told that Elizabeth was barren. There is not a hint that Zechariah could have been infertile. Throughout the early years of her marriage, Elizabeth would have been hoping and praying that she would become pregnant; but each month that hope was dashed. As the years went by, her hope would have given way to anxiety and then panic, until finally she reached an age when she knew she would never conceive.

Zechariah was a direct descendant of Aaron and that made him a priest automatically. There could have been as many as 20,000 priests in Jesus' day, which was far more than the Temple needed. The priests' duties were drawn by lots and many of them would never once get the privilege of (for example) burning incense on the altar of the Temple, before the morning sacrifice or after the evening sacrifice. Any ordinary priest whose name *was* called would surely regard that day as the greatest of his life. One day, the lottery finally selects Zechariah to be the priest to go into the Temple and offer incense before God. His job is to place the incense (which represents the people's prayers) on the hot altar and then prostrate himself, while the congregation outside recites these words: 'May the merciful God enter the Holy Place and accept with favour the offering of His people.'

Zechariah's big day arrives and all is going well until suddenly Gabriel appears. Understandably, Zechariah is scared rigid. This is the last thing he expected to happen! But Gabriel tells him not to be afraid. Although at the altar Zechariah is praying for the whole nation, God has a personal message just for him. The angel then tells him that his prayer has been heard. Now, you can imagine Zechariah thinking: Which prayer? It's very unlikely that he has prayed this morning for Elizabeth to become pregnant. In fact, he probably gave up praying for that ages ago, once she had become too old to conceive.

Gabriel continues: 'Elizabeth will bear you a son, and you are to call him John. He will be a joy and delight to you, and many will rejoice because of his birth, for he will be great in the sight of the Lord. He is never to take wine or other fermented drink, and he will be filled with the Holy Spirit even before he is born. He will bring back many of the people of Israel to the Lord their God. And he will go on before the Lord, in the spirit and power of Elijah … to make ready a people prepared for the Lord' (Luke 1:13–17).

Now, although of course this is brilliant news, I wonder whether Zechariah's first reaction is really one of excitement. I've noticed that the older I get, the more set in my ways I become. I don't want things to upset my daily routine. I wonder whether a message delivered to an old man out of the blue saying that he is about to start a family and have a baby in his home would really make him jump for joy.

Zechariah is understandably stunned and doubts what the angel is saying. 'How can I be sure of this?' he asks. Like Abraham before him, his hopes of a child perished a long time ago. He is an old man and Elizabeth is an old woman. He was completely unprepared for what he has just been told. 'Listen,' says Gabriel. 'I stand in the presence of God and He has sent me here to bring you this good news.' Because Zechariah has not believed his message, he adds, he will not be able to speak another word until the day it comes true.

Now, while all this has been going on, the congregation outside must have been getting worried. Zechariah has been in the Holy Place far longer than expected. When he finally does appear, I guess that everyone assumes that whatever has happened inside the Holy Place, Zechariah has been struck dumb by the shock. What happens next has been described by Tom Wright as a dark comedy. 'How would you describe seeing an angel to a waiting crowd of people,' he writes in *Luke for Everyone*, 'by just using your hands and arms?' I also wonder how Zechariah convinces Elizabeth in mime that she will become pregnant.

Also, we must remember that, unlike with Mary, this is not going to be an immaculate conception! How does he persuade Elizabeth that they should have an early night and that if she says she has a headache she is actually going against God's will?

Nonetheless, just as Gabriel said, the impossible does happen. Elizabeth becomes pregnant and for a while she hides herself away in seclusion. Although she must be thrilled, she may be slightly embarrassed by people seeing her, an old lady with morning sickness, or staring at her as she grows bigger. Maybe she is even frightened she may lose the baby. But after five months she is confident that God has indeed performed a miracle; and by the time the pregnant Mary calls, she is receiving visitors.

Eventually, the boy is born. Eight days later, he is ready for circumcision but still, we are told, Zechariah is unable to speak. (The Bible also says that people now communicate with him with signs, which may indicate that he is also deaf.) Custom dictates that the boy should be named after his father, but Elizabeth insists that he must be called John. The relatives and neighbours protest. No one else in the family has that name! So, they turn to Zechariah and ask him in sign language, hoping they will get more sense out of him. Zechariah writes on a tablet: 'His name is John.' At this moment, he is at last able to speak again and he praises God with the wonderful words of what the Prayer Book calls 'the Benedictus' (Luke 1:68–79).

So, to conclude. People try and convince me as I get older that the best is yet to come; but I find that hard to believe. In the 1980s and '90s, I was in big demand and got invited to minister all around the world. TV channels wanted me, and my book and album sales were in their thousands. Nowadays, the invitations are fewer and the sales are far fewer. What I do has changed. A lot of my time is spent talking to and befriending both believers and not-yet-believers. I also visit my old leukaemia ward at least once a week as a chaplain, where I pray for and try to encourage people struggling with cancer.

As we get older things do change; but that doesn't mean they are less valuable. Although the past may have been good for my ego, I'm beginning to realise that the way God is using me now, with relatively few people, could be even more significant than standing in front of very large audiences. So long as we are alive and breathing, God still has a plan for our lives. And whatever age we have reached, I believe He still has some special surprises in store for us. We can never retire from His service, although He may move us on into new pastures to continue to serve Him.

So, hang on in there, because there is still a work for Jesus that no one but you can do!

⟩ The evil emperor

KEY VERSE

'You know for yourselves that we're not much to look at. We've been surrounded and battered by troubles, but we're not demoralized; we're not sure what to do, but we know that God knows what to do; we've been spiritually terrorized, but God hasn't left our side; we've been thrown down, but we haven't broken … While we're going through the worst, you're getting in on the best!' 2 Corinthians 4:7–9,12 (The Message)

HE WAS BORN in AD 37. Historians inform us that he was fair-haired with weak blue eyes, had a fat neck, a pot belly and a body which smelt and was covered with spots. He usually appeared in public in a sort of dressing gown without a belt, a scarf round his neck and no shoes. In character, he was a strange, even paradoxical mix: artistic, sporting, brutal, weak, sensual, erratic, extravagant, sadistic, bisexual – and, later in life, almost certainly deranged. In his younger, saner days, he considered making big changes to his empire. His radical ideas included ending the killing of gladiators and condemned criminals as a public spectacle. In fact, at first this emperor – due largely to the influence of his wise tutor Seneca, most likely – came across as a very humane ruler. Later, however, he even forced wise old Seneca to commit suicide. What corrupted him was mainly his extreme lust and his lack of self-control. His desires ruled him!

His mother, Agrippina, was a controlling woman who had always wanted more control over both him and the Empire – so in return he made various attempts on her life. Three times he tried to poison her, and when that didn't work he tried rigging the ceiling over her bed to collapse while she lay in it. Again, no joy. He then went to the trouble of having a collapsible boat made that was meant to sink in the Bay of Naples. But the plot succeeded only in sinking the boat – Agrippina managed to swim ashore. Finally, in exasperation, the Emperor sent an assassin who clubbed and stabbed her to death. He celebrated by staging yet wilder orgies, and creating two new festivals of chariot-racing and athletics.

He also loved being on stage and so he arranged musical contests, which gave him further opportunity to demonstrate in public his talent for singing while accompanying himself on the lyre. Remember that this was a time when actors and other performers were regarded as rather unsavoury. It was a moral outrage to have an emperor showing off on stage. Worse still, he passed a law that no one was allowed to leave the auditorium, for any reason whatever, while he was performing. The historian Suetonius writes of women giving birth during the Emperor's recitals, and of men pretending to die just so they could be carried out and escape.

He married a woman called Poppaea Sabina, but she, too, was later killed. Suetonius says that the Emperor kicked her to death when she complained at his coming home late from the races. Then, in July 64, a great fire ravaged the city for six days. This was when he was famously supposed to have 'fiddled while Rome burned'. The historian Dio Cassius tells us how he 'climbed onto the palace roof, from which there was the best overall view of the greater part of the fire, and sang "The Capture of Troy"'. Whether or not this story was true, the rumour was enough to make people suspect that his efforts to put out the fire had not been genuine. Many people think that he wanted Rome destroyed so that he could build a new capital and name it after himself.

However, the Emperor didn't want to be blamed for the fire as he always craved popularity, and so he looked for a scapegoat. He found it in an obscure religious sect new to Rome: Christians. So, in 64 he had them all rounded up and then proceeded to inflict on them some of the worst atrocities in recorded history. He didn't want just to kill Christians; he wanted to make them suffer first. He enjoyed having them dipped in wax and then impaled on poles around his palace. He would then set them on fire and yell: 'Now you truly *are* the light of the world!' Often, he had Christians killed in the Circus Maximus in front of large audiences. He would have men and women wrapped in animal skins and thrown to lions or dogs who would then tear them apart. Others he had crucified and then, if the spectators got bored, set on fire. This makes hard reading but it needs to be said. We must never forget how our brothers and sisters suffered in those early days of Christianity. Our faith has come down to us through the blood of martyrs.

On a pilgrimage to Rome, I visited one of the catacombs where about half a million Christians were buried, including many children and young people. I found it very challenging seeing these underground chambers that go on for miles. The amazing thing is that above some of the shelves where the bodies were laid you can still see the remains of some brightly coloured artwork. Far from being scared of death, these people seem to have celebrated it because they believed that, once they had left this earth, the very next person they met would be the Lord Jesus, for whom they had lived and died. We have no idea how many Christians lost their lives in this persecution, but this emperor continued victimising Christians for several years, not only in Rome but throughout the Empire. So, we can be sure that a very large number of Christians lost their lives in this period.

However, this strategy backfired. Many Romans who had been 'anti-Christian' turned against the Emperor because of the torture he inflicted on the followers of this new faith. Many of them even became believers when they saw how genuine the martyrs were. Far from eradicating the new faith, the Emperor helped to bring about a revival. It was this brutality, though, that established him as the first Antichrist in the eyes of the Church. The persecution would go on for 200 years.

As he grew ever more excessive and even more mad, the Senate could see that Rome was in danger and it condemned the Emperor to be flogged to death. When he heard this, he took the coward's way out and chose rather to commit suicide, which he did with the help of a secretary on 9 June 68. His last words were: *Qualis artifex pereo*! ('What an artist dies in me!')

Of course, by now you know I have been talking about the Emperor Nero Claudius Caesar. What is most incredible, though, is the apostle Paul's driving ambition to share the good news of Jesus with one of the most evil men on earth! When Paul faced Festus, who worked for Nero, and Agrippa II, the King of Palestine, they both recognised that he was innocent and they would have let him go free. But Paul insisted as a Roman citizen that he should be sent to Rome to be tried by none other than the Emperor Nero himself. He relished the chance to preach the good news of Jesus to those in the highest of places. And both Festus and Agrippa knew they could not stop him.

We know that after a long and arduous journey Paul did eventually arrive in Rome. There he was kept under guard for two years before the Emperor finally heard his case. Did Paul really stand before Nero? Neither the Bible nor the history books tell us, but I am convinced that he did. God's messengers do not lie and the angel told Paul in Acts 27:24, 'You must stand trial before Caesar'.

The great apostle won his appeal, only to be condemned later by one of the most despicable pieces of human flesh ever to disgrace this planet. According to the historian Eusebius, Nero had Paul beheaded and Peter crucified. A tragic way for their lives to end? Neither Paul nor Peter would have thought so. They had completed the work Jesus had asked them to do on earth and now it was time to rejoin Him – forever!

Joy? You're having a laugh!

KEY VERSE *'I've told you these things for a purpose: that my joy might be your joy, and your joy wholly mature.' John 15:11 (The Message)*

AFTER THE CHURCH service, a little boy told the vicar: 'When I grow up, I'm going to give you some money.'

'Well, thank you,' said the vicar. 'But why?'

The boy replied: 'Because my daddy says you're one of the poorest preachers we've ever had.'

Everyone likes a joke. Everyone likes to laugh. Or should I say: Everyone *needs* to laugh. A health-and-fitness website informs us:

'The sound of roaring laughter is far more contagious than any cough, sniffle, or sneeze. When laughter is shared, it binds people together and increases happiness and intimacy. In addition to the domino effect of joy and amusement, laughter also triggers healthy physical changes in the body. Humour and laughter strengthen your immune system, boost your energy, diminish pain, and protect you from the damaging effects of stress.'

Life is very tough for some of us, though, and gives us very little to laugh about. However, in John 16:20 Jesus promises: 'Your grief will turn to joy.'

'Joy' is a word rarely used nowadays except in church circles, yet it must be a fairly important word as it is used over 200 times in the Bible. *Webster's New World Dictionary* says 'joyful' is synonymous with 'happy', 'glad' and 'cheerful'. It has largely been replaced by 'happy' nowadays, but do these two words really mean the same thing? In the Bible, joy may be a state of happiness but it is a special gift to those who are believers. It is very much part of a person's faith, an announcement of the saving power of God. According to this definition, joy can relate to praise and thanksgiving in public worship or to quiet personal meditation.

In the Old Testament, joy is often expressed physically. Singing, shouting, uproar, noisy instruments, a loud voice, dancing, clapping, leaping, stamping the feet, all are associated with manifestations of joy. But that is the expression of joy, not joy itself. Although joy includes happiness, it is also very different from happiness. For the follower of Jesus, joy is the happy state that results from knowing and serving God.

Joy is repeatedly shown to be the natural outcome of fellowship with God. 'In your presence there is fullness of joy,' says Psalm 16:11 (NRSV). In the New Testament we read of the 'good tidings of great joy' that constitute the gospel. Joy is certainly something that Jesus both taught about and demonstrated. In spite of the grief and tragedy in His life, His behaviour was joyful, a contrast with the strict, miserable faces and lifestyles of the Jewish religious leaders around Him.

Defending His disciples for not fasting, Jesus described Himself as a bridegroom. He enjoyed eating and drinking, which allowed people to accuse Him of being a glutton and a drunk. He enjoyed socialising and sharing meals with people, and even though He had only three years to save the world He still found time to attend a wedding in Cana. And joy is a feature of many of the parables. The man who discovered the buried treasure was filled with joy. The stories of the lost sheep, the lost coin and the lost son all conclude with God and His angels rejoicing over sinners who repent. In the parable of the talents, the servant who used his talents wisely was told to come and share 'the joy of the Lord' that was the reward for his faithfulness.

Jesus was very keen to pass on His joy to His followers. One of the greatest verses on joy is John 16:22, where Jesus speaks words of encouragement to His disciples. He tells them that the grief and sorrow they are enduring now is temporary but joy is permanent and no one can take it away. In the dark days of disappointment that succeeded His crucifixion, the joy of the disciples may have been hard to see, but at the resurrection and on the Day of Pentecost their exuberant joy was very evident. Afterwards, it remained a marked characteristic of the Early Church, even through very difficult periods of persecution. It seems that before the disciples experienced great joy, there was great grief and sorrow. Maybe it's only when we have experienced true grief that we find true joy.

Of course, being joyful doesn't mean we will always have a 24/7 'Cheshire cat' grin on our faces. Sometimes they will show sadness, pain and (dare I say?) even depression, because we are human. But if we consistently have faces as miserable as sin and still proclaim to non-believers that we have 'the joy of the Lord', they may not be convinced. They may even prefer to remain non-believers with happy faces!

So, biblical joy is bound up with our relationship with Jesus. Although there is much we do not understand, we do know that we have been forgiven and have a place in His purpose because His Spirit lives within us. Jesus declared that no one could take away our joy. Joy comes from God and our walk with Him, so as believers no one can take away the joy of our salvation. Which means that our joy will be complete as we seek to fulfil God's will for us here on earth. At the end, we all want to hear His words, 'Well done, good and faithful servant. Enter into the joy of your Lord.'

Let me adapt an Oscar Wilde quote: 'Some Christians cause happiness wherever they go; others whenever they go.' In a lost, broken world so full of confusion and sadness, people don't just need jokers and comedians to give them temporary laughter. One of the first songs I wrote after becoming a Christian had these lyrics:

'We've got Jesus, we've got joy
We've got Jesus, we've got joy
We've got something that we want to share with you
We've got Jesus, we've got joy
We've got Jesus, we've got joy
And we hope some day that you will find Him too.'

I believed it then as a baby Christian, and guess what? I still believe it today! I pray that as believers we can cause happiness wherever we go and so can direct people to the source of our true joy: Jesus.

A good mark!

KEY VERSE *'Treat everyone you meet with dignity. Love your spiritual family.' 1 Peter 2:17 (The Message)*

JOHN MARK WAS a son of Mary, a leading Christian who lived just outside Jerusalem. They must have lived in a rather large house, as it's likely that Jesus and the disciples used it for meetings and prayer and so did the Early Church. John Mark was probably a teenager throughout Jesus' three-year ministry and would more than likely have been around whenever a special meeting was held in the upper room of his house. He also seems to have got on very well with Peter, as we shall see later.

'A young man, wearing nothing but a linen garment, was following Jesus. When they seized him, he fled naked, leaving his garment behind' (Mark 14:51–52). Many theologians would agree that this is our first introduction to John Mark himself. His is the only Gospel that mentions this incident, which both Matthew and Luke, who took a lot of their content from his writings, omit as unimportant.

Let me give you a possible prelude to this strange Bible verse, although it can't be proved one way or the other. Supposing, as is widely thought, the Last Supper was actually held in John Mark's mum's house. The room would have been upstairs with steps going up to it. John Mark would have been with his mum below. He would have heard, or maybe even seen, Judas leaving early (after Satan had entered him, as John's Gospel says). It's late and he's in bed. Suddenly, there's a noise at the door! Judas and the Temple police are outside, expecting to find Jesus there; but Jesus has already left for Gethsemane. John Mark leaps out of bed and rushes out to try and find Jesus to warn Him. By the time he does find Him, it's too late. Some of the arresting party try to seize him, too, and as he escapes, his flimsy nightclothes are torn off, leaving him both scared and naked.

Whatever happened that night, I believe that John Mark included this detail to prove that he was there at the arrest of Jesus and that he was too terrified to stay with Him. He ran for his life, just as his friend Peter was to deny three times that he knew Jesus. Maybe there is one crucial difference between the young man and the older apostle: we know that after his denials Peter broke down and wept, and we know he was never to make the same mistake again. After Jesus was crucified and had risen again from the dead, the disciples continued to meet in John Mark's house, and we can be sure that as he grew older he continued to spend time with them.

Then we jump forward to Acts 13. We are now in Antioch, about 300 miles away from Jerusalem. Barnabas and the new convert Saul are chosen to take the good news of Jesus to the whole world. Barnabas was certainly the senior Christian of the two – it was he who befriended and trusted Saul and introduced him to the other disciples when everyone else was still scared of him. So, it seems that Barnabas was the leader of the tour – and, being the leader, he chose to go to Cyprus, his native island, first. John Mark was his cousin and he went with Barnabas and Saul as their assistant. There the young man must have witnessed a good deal of sexual immorality, as Paphos was famous for the worship of Venus, the goddess of love. It was on Cyprus, too, that Saul first became known as Paul.

After this, however, things went sour for John Mark. Something happened and while Paul and Barnabas travelled on, he headed back to Jerusalem. What caused this rift between the young man and the two older apostles? Maybe, unlike Peter, he had not learned his lesson at Gethsemane and he got scared and ran off home. Or maybe, being a good Jew, he had theological problems with preaching to the Gentiles. Or maybe he was just a young man who was homesick. Or maybe he couldn't cope with Paul's leadership ...

Up until that point, it had always been 'Barnabas and Saul' (that's the way it's written in our Bibles), but after Cyprus it is nearly always 'Paul and Barnabas', with Paul taking the lead. Barnabas was a humble, godly man and had no problems with this, but the young John Mark may have thought that Paul should have remained number two to his more experienced uncle. Maybe he wasn't going to be under Paul's authority, made his feelings known to the new team leader a]nd quit.

Paul wasn't perfect and, being human, let his feelings about John Mark be known to some of the leaders of the churches he visited. From now on, it was going to be very hard for the young man to live with what had happened. When he got back to Jerusalem, people – not least his family! – would have wanted to know why he had returned so soon. He must have lost all his self-respect and felt a failure. That would have been enough to make some people give up the faith altogether, but not John Mark – though, like most of us, he may have considered it once or twice.

In Acts 15, we read that Paul and Barnabas, having travelled a long way together, were now back in Antioch, about to embark on another tour of the cities they had visited. Barnabas wanted to give John Mark another chance and ask him to join them, but Paul would not accept a deserter and, maybe, someone who had not submitted to his leadership earlier.

John Mark also proved to be a cause of division between the two apostles. Argument and disagreement broke out between them, so much so that they parted company and (as far as we know) never travelled with each other again. Understandably, Paul didn't want a weak link to mess up the mission, while Barnabas was willing to give the young man, perhaps because he was family, another chance. So, Paul hooked up with Silas and Barnabas went with John Mark. And, so far as we can tell, God blessed both teams.

It seems that John Mark, having lost his relationship with one of the Church's most senior apostles, Paul, went back and hung out with its other most senior apostle, Peter. We know he spent a lot of time with Peter because Mark's Gospel is really the mind and memory of Peter.

John Mark's story could have ended there and being with Peter and writing his Gospel would have made it a wonderful failure-to-success story. But no, there's more! Years after the big fall-out, we find Paul imprisoned in Rome for the first time. He is to spend at least two years under house arrest. And who do we find sitting with him? John Mark. We don't know how it happened, we don't even have any idea of who initiated it, but happen it did. Paul writes to Philemon about John Mark being one of his fellow workers.

Some time later, we discover from 2 Timothy that Paul has again been imprisoned, this time by the Christian-hating Emperor Nero. In contrast to his first imprisonment, he is now in a cold, damp dungeon, chained up like a criminal. He knows his life is nearly over, and he is very lonely. He writes to his spiritual son, Timothy, and asks him to come and see him soon. He talks about Demas, who has deserted him. In the next sentence, he asks Timothy to bring John Mark with him when he comes. Why? Because he's just the sort of person Paul wants with him in the short time he has left on this earth. No more thoughts of a deserter. Paul wants his closest friends around him in these last days – and maybe, never having met Jesus in the flesh himself, enjoys especially the company of someone who knew Him well. For years the young man needed the older apostles, but now things have changed and this older apostle needs the young man.

A short while later, both Peter and Paul would have been martyred. God is not ageist and has no preference for either young or old people. He will use anyone of any age who is obedient to Him. I believe that there does need to be more love, honour and respect flowing both ways between younger and older Christians. We really do need each other if we are serious about completing the tasks God has planned for us to do while we are here on earth. The old have got experience of life to pass on; the young have the energy to get out and pass it on!

A law unto themselves

'Now that the time for faith is here, the Law is no longer in charge of us.' Galatians 3:25 (GNB)

GALATIANS HAS BEEN referred to as Paul's hottest letter – the Magna Carta of Christian liberty. Martin Luther and John Bunyan both had a high regard for the blunt language used in this letter. Paul is fighting on two fronts: the opposite dangers of licence and legalism. Both take away freedom and return a person to slavery. We either become a slave to our own wrong desires or we become a slave to the Law and the rules of others. Although this subject is a feast of a debate, please allow me to feed you just a tiny takeaway to chew over as Paul tries to define law and grace.

Being brought up in a Christian community, my teaching on law and grace was very pick'n'mix. I was taught that I needed to obey only ten of the 613 laws that God gave to the Jews via Moses. But even those ten 'commandments' had been given a modern spin so that they sort of fitted in with today's culture and my evangelical Christian upbringing. For instance, the Fourth Commandment: 'Remember the Sabbath day by keeping it holy.' As a child, I was taught that the Sabbath was on a Saturday. I couldn't understand how come we had now changed it to a Sunday. Where and when in the New Testament did this switch take place? Who said it was now God's plan that Sunday should be observed as the Christian Sabbath?

Fortunately, I only had to obey a few, carefully selected Sabbath rules. The vast majority of the regulations recorded in the Old Testament were ignored for some reason. On Sundays, I was not allowed to watch any 'worldly' television programmes. These, of course, were the ones my school buddies were enjoying and would be talking about in the break on Monday. I was the odd one out. Exceptions were made, though, and the box could be switched on for boring adult programmes such as the news (as well as religious programmes, of course). No worldly sport could be watched, either on TV or live – and definitely not if it would involve an admission charge. There was no worldly buying of ice creams (even if it was a boiling hot sunny day), and of course no worldly newspapers.

By and large, I was not allowed anything that encouraged people to work on a Sunday. Strangely enough, it was all right to buy a newspaper on Monday, although even as a small boy I was pretty sure that Monday's paper had been put together and even printed the day before. I was never given a proper answer when I questioned whether it was right to attend a church service on a Sunday. As a child, I thought: Not only is it a place where we have to pay an admission charge in the form of our weekly tithe, but also, surely, we are encouraging the vicar to work on a Sunday. How can that be right?

My parents were very grateful for the Fifth Commandment, 'Honour your father and your mother' – and fortunately the community only stuck to the Exodus basics. I was pleased that it chose not to apply the further teaching of Moses which unpacks and expands the commandment in Deuteronomy 21, stating that a child who does not obey their parents should be dragged before the elders and then stoned to death.

I appreciate that, as Paul points out, there are Christians who have taken liberty to extremes, but there are also many Christians who are still trying to live the life of a Pharisee, sticking rigidly to certain Mosaic laws and yet to discover grace and true freedom. Theirs is often a life of 'Thou shalt not', and sadly they tend not to be fun people. To put it another way, they are not people I personally would choose to go on holiday with!

So, what was the point of the 613 Old Testament laws? They were meant to be about people demonstrating the reign of God in every aspect of their lives, in faithfulness to their covenant with Him. For Christians, that is demonstrated by our faithfulness to Christ, but we could be challenged on whether the details of our lives actually bear this out.

Someone has given this simple illustration.

In the Greek world of the New Testament, many families had a special household servant.

He was usually an old and trusted slave who had been with the family for a long time and whose character and standards were very good. He was not a schoolmaster, but he was responsible for the children's moral welfare. He had to keep an eye on the children and keep them out of temptation or danger, and make sure that they acquired the qualities essential to true adulthood. He had one particular duty: every day, he had to take the children to and from school. He had nothing to do with the teaching of the children, he just had to take them safely to the school and deliver them to the teacher.

This is similar to the function of the Law. The Law is there to lead a person to Christ. It can't take them into Christ's presence but it can get them to a place from which they can find their way into His presence themselves. The Law is there to make sinful people *feel* sinful, feel failures. The Law is there to make bad people feel bad. Is it ever possible for a sinful, bad person to feel good? Praise God, yes! Jesus the Messiah came to earth and lived a perfect life, died upon a cross and rose again so that at last sinful people might have the chance not just to feel good but to have their sins actually forgiven and to be made right with God.

At last the answer to the Law had arrived. Romans 10:4 reveals that Christ is the end of the Law. This being the case, Paul informs us, once someone becomes a follower of Jesus they no longer need the Law, for from now on they will rely not on keeping laws but receiving grace. Paul says that he himself is not under the Law, and nor is any other Christian. All of us are now under grace – the undeserved love of God. He goes on to say that everyone who has been baptised into Christ has clothed themselves with Christ.

The early Christians regarded baptism not merely as an outward ceremony but as something that resulted in real union, real oneness, with Christ. The baptised were almost literally 'clothed' with Christ. In the Early Church, each baptismal candidate was given a loose-fitting, pure white robe. As they put it on, it was a symbol that they were 'putting on' Christ. One result of this was that everyone being baptised looked much the same. As they 'put on' Christ, there was no difference in appearance between any of the candidates, whether they were Jews or Greeks, slaves or free people, male or female. They all became 'sons of God'.

In a song I wrote long ago called 'Father God, I Wonder', there's a line that goes: 'Now I am your son, I am adopted in your family.' I took that from Galatians 3:28, but over the years I have got a lot of grief for it. Some songbooks have changed the word 'son' to 'child'. My point was that in this context there is neither male nor female and we are all sons of God because biblically it's the sons who inherit the kingdom. Some women were furious that I – or the Bible – should refer to them as sons. I would try to calm them down by explaining that God is totally fair: He may refer to females as 'sons' but He also refers to males as 'brides'!

Paul insists that the distinction between Jews and Greeks, slaves and free people, male and female has been erased. Before he became a Christian, Paul would have been a strict observer of the Jewish form of morning prayer.

There is a thanksgiving where a Jew thanks God that 'You have not made me a Gentile, a slave or a woman'. That is what is so amazing about this scripture. Paul has the nerve to take this prayer that all his Jewish readers would know and contradict it. The old distinctions are gone with the old Law.

Grace demands that there should be unity where there had been disunity, communion where there had been division. From now on, the Church of Jesus is going to be 'all one'. It is only when we fully realise that no one is superior, that we are all sinners saved by grace, that we will truly understand that all believers are 'all one in Christ Jesus'.

Read it again Ian — d make
Some necessary distinctions
between Jews & Gentile!

❯ A hearing problem

KEY VERSE *'Ask and you'll get.' Luke 11:9 (The Message)*

IN THE ELEVENTH century BC, a young woman from the hill country married a man called Elkanah. She longed to conceive and give birth to a child, but this was just not happening. What made things worse was that Elkanah had also married another wife, called Peninnah, and she was very fertile. Not only was she happy and able to give Elkanah plenty of children but also she was happy and able to give poor Hannah a hard time because she couldn't get pregnant. Elkanah really loved Hannah and gave her special treats, but this was no consolation for not being able to conceive! She was so upset, both by the fact she was childless and by the constant taunting from Peninnah, she would starve herself of food and spend a lot of time in tears. Elkanah tried to help matters by saying that surely he meant more to her than having ten sons but, as often happens when someone really wants something, no amount of reasoning could change Hannah's mind. She was inconsolable.

One day, while on a pilgrimage to Shiloh, she lingered in the 'Lord's house', crying as she prayed. She thought she would try to bargain with God and promised that if He gave her a son, she would give him back to the Lord for all the days of his life. The elderly priest Eli was sitting by the doorway and, seeing Hannah's lips moving but hearing no sound coming out, he assumed she was drunk. He told her to give up the wine if she couldn't control herself, but Hannah insisted that she hadn't been drinking and wasn't drunk, she was just pouring her heart out before God because she was so full of sadness. Eli told her to go in peace and prayed that the Lord would answer her prayers. Hannah left feeling happier and had some food. It seems that God had revealed to her that her prayers would indeed be answered. They were, and she soon conceived and gave birth to a very special little boy whom she named Samuel.

Hannah knew she had promised God that she would give her little boy back to Him, so when he was still very young he went to work in the 'Lord's house' with the high priest, Eli, who was by now very old and going blind. One night, after a long day, Eli had turned in and was asleep in his usual place, while the boy Samuel slept in the 'Lord's house'. When all was still and quiet, Samuel suddenly heard someone calling his name. He thought that Eli must need him, so he ran to where the old man was sleeping and said: 'Here I am. Did you call me?' Old Eli obviously needed his sleep and I don't think he was too happy about being woken up in the middle of the night by an excitable young boy. He told him to go back to bed. Just as the boy was dozing off again, he heard the same voice calling: 'Samuel! Samuel!' Again he ran back and woke up old Eli saying, 'Here I am! Didn't you call me?' Nobody likes a broken night's sleep and, having been woken up twice, I dare say Eli was not that happy about it either. 'My son,' he said, 'I did not call you. Now, please go back to sleep.' The Bible here explains that at this stage Samuel didn't know the Lord and 'the word of the Lord had not yet been revealed to him'.

Back he went to bed and then, as before, just as he was getting to sleep, he heard the same voice for the third time, calling his name. By now, even Samuel must have felt a bit nervous about waking old Eli up for the third time; but he genuinely believed he must have called his name because he needed some sort of help. So, once again he ran to Eli saying: 'Here I am! You did call me, didn't you?' Something at last was starting to twig in the old priest's head. If *he* hadn't been calling Samuel, maybe it was God! It had been a long time since God had spoken to anyone and Eli clearly wasn't expecting anyone to hear His voice – especially not a young lad like Samuel. Anyway, he instructed the boy to return to his bed and if he heard the voice again, to reply: 'Speak, Lord, for Your servant is listening.'

Sure enough, the voice again called, 'Samuel! Samuel!' and this time Samuel responded just as Eli had told him to. Then God said to the boy: 'I am about to do something in Israel that will make the ears of everyone who hears it tingle.' He also said that Eli and his two sons had not pleased Him and would be punished. (Eli was a very godly man but he had allowed his sons to serve as priests even though he knew they were degenerate men.)

In the morning, Samuel was not particularly keen to see Eli because he knew he would want to know if God had spoken to him and what exactly He had said. He was a bit frightened to pass on the message because it certainly did not contain good news for Eli. Then he heard his name being called again and this time he knew it was Eli. The high priest insisted that Samuel tell him everything and said that if he held anything back, God would punish him. Samuel told him everything. Eli just said: 'He is the Lord; let Him do what is good in His eyes.' I wonder why he resigned himself to the fact that this was a fait accompli? Why didn't he try and sort things out – sacking and punishing his sons for a starter, and then crying out to God for mercy?

So, let me finish by looking at the remarkable difference between Hannah and Eli. The Bible says that it was God who 'closed Hannah's womb'. It would have been so easy for her to just leave it there and enjoy her husband's love. No way! She was going to starve herself, cry loads and spend time with God pleading for Him to change her situation. As we have seen, she was even willing to do a deal with Him if He let her have a son.

Eli, however, did nothing. Hannah's prayer was answered. In fact, she went on to have five more children, although none of them could match the first, miracle child whom she gave back to God. Samuel was special to God. He was special to Hannah. He is special to us, as we can still learn so much from this man in Scripture.

When I am asking God for something, I sometimes feel that His answer is 'no' and the more I keep asking, the more I feel sure that what I am asking for is not going to happen. I may not understand why He is saying no, but, being God, He always gets the last word because He only does what is best. But if I pray and I *don't* seem to hear a reply, that is when, like Hannah, I'm going to keep on asking until He does answer. More often than not, He allows me to have what I've asked for – but it may take a few asks!

Singing from the same song sheet

KEY VERSE

'Summing up: Be agreeable, be sympathetic, be loving, be compassionate, be humble. That goes for all of you, no exceptions.' 1 Peter 3:8 (The Message)

I THINK ENGLISH must be a very difficult language to learn. Often, words have more than one meaning. For example, I love playing and watching golf. For someone learning English, it must be very hard to grasp that not only can you join a golf club, you can also use a golf club to hit a small white ball.

The word 'church' has quite a few different meanings. It can refer to a building we see or a service we attend (as in 'I'm going to church'), or there's the New Testament meaning of 'the Body of Christ' or 'God's called-out-to-be-together people'.

A few years ago, my publisher, CWR, had a competition in their *Topz* children's daily reading booklet. Twenty children won the first prize, which was an invitation to sing two songs in a recording studio which would then be produced into a single. I was commissioned to write the songs and to produce and oversee the recording. Now, I'm a firm believer that not only has Britain got talent but also our Christian children have talent; but just because they win a competition doesn't mean their talent is necessarily singing.

The day of the recording came. The lucky winners were in the studio, their very proud parents gazing and waving at them through a soundproof window. After one take, I realised that these children were never going to manage to sing in unison, let alone harmony – and there was definitely at least one little growler hidden away among them. The only solution: good singers right next to the microphone, not-so-good singers nowhere near the microphone. And growlers nowhere near the good singers! A thumbs up to the parents through the glass to say their kids are brilliant, then … hope for the best! The recording didn't exactly have the quality of a good choir, but the single was enjoyed by many, although I'm guessing that most of those who enjoyed it were related in some way to the children singing on it!

Far more important than vocal harmony is church unity and harmony. In John 17, Jesus prays that believers may be as one as He and His Father are one. Now, does that mean that Jesus wants all His followers to think the same, interpret the Bible the same and even look the same, so we all end up like those little Homepride flour graders? I think not.

I often wonder why Jesus, when selecting His twelve disciples, didn't choose nice, relaxed, easy-to-get-on-with people. Let's face it, He really did pick a weird bunch. It's easy to see why the religious leaders of the day questioned His wisdom in choosing such men when I'm sure there was a far more intelligent, reliable and just *better* class of disciple He could have gone for. Perhaps He thought: If I can get this motley crew to love each other, maybe there will be hope for the Church in years to come!

Paul, too, felt very strongly about the importance of Christian unity. To the Christians in Rome he writes, 'Just as the body is one and has many members, and all the members of the body, though many, are one body, so it is with Christ' (1 Cor. 12:12, NRSV), and he pleads with them to be of one mind. He tells the Christians in Corinth to stop their quarrelling and be of one mind. Because they have shared in one bread, they must be one body and must live in peace with each other.

To the Christians in Ephesus he writes that Christians must maintain the unity of the Spirit, remembering that there is one Lord, one faith, one baptism and one God and Father of all. And he tells the Christians in Philippi that if they want to make his happiness complete they must stand fast in one spirit, striving together with one mind, for the faith of the gospel, and they must love one another. I wonder, if Paul was still writing letters today, what he would say to the churches to which you and I belong …

The New Testament teaches that Christian unity is not an optional extra. No one can truly live the Christian life unless they are actively trying to show love to those around them. In our reading, Peter reminds us of the importance of unity. He pleads for Christians to have unity of spirit, sympathy, love for one another, a tender heart and a humble mind. There were factions in the Early Church – those who followed Paul, those who followed Apollos and so on – but they didn't seem to have the very disparate denominations we have today.

I believe a book was once published called *Forgive Us Our Denominations*, but denominations in themselves are not a bad thing. I think it's wonderful that believers have such a varied choice of how and where to worship. There are church services to suit every taste. There are styles to suit those who appreciate the sacramental and traditional and styles to suit those who enjoy the lively and informal. None is better or worse than the others and as long as God is being truly worshipped, I believe that He enjoys them all. But, sadly, many Christians don't. It's almost second nature to criticise or even mock those who don't do things our way. It makes us feel our church is superior, more spiritual, even closer to God than other churches in the area.

Many years ago when I arrived to pastor a Pentecostal church in Lancashire, I was informed that the local Baptist church had a good minister but they didn't have the Holy Spirit. Christian unity has to be a lot deeper than everyone just holding hands in a big circle and singing 'Bind Us Together, Lord', like some of us did many years ago. My travelling evangelistic ministry takes me to all denominations, not just Anglican churches. Each year, I have the privilege of ministering to the Baptists, Methodists and Free Churches and even church gatherings that meet in schools, village halls and pubs. Of course, we all have our particular preference for how church should be and what we should do in our services; but as no denomination has all the answers, it's so important that we stay open-minded and willing to learn from those who love Jesus but do things differently from us.

Let me finish where I began. A church leader once told me that his church would be perfect if it wasn't for the people – but it is people that Jesus chose to make up His Church, not stones or services. My friend Gordon Bailey, the poet, writes:

'Why are some churches derided,
And others decidedly odd?
Well, I've thought it through and decided
To pin the blame squarely on God.
He could have built churches of stone, slate, and pews
With chancel, and turret, and steeple;
Yet, with so much to choose, and so much to lose,
He went and made churches of people.'

Sadly, instead of portraying the beautiful Body of Christ on earth, we often portray the opposite. I wonder how many seekers are put off from following Jesus just by observing the arguments and disputes between different churches. Of course, you and I are not in a position to sort out the problem of worldwide church unity, but maybe we can do a little to bring a bit more unity to our area. How? Well, we could start quite simply by respecting and honouring those Christians around us who believe different things and worship in different ways. We know we must try to love the unchurched, but do we realise that we must also love the churched? Which can sometimes be even more of a challenge. Everyone should know we are Christians not by the fact that we attend church but by the fact that we are loving.

Naaman the old water baby

KEY VERSE

'If all you do is love the lovable, do you expect a bonus? Anybody can do that.' Matthew 5:46 (The Message)

LET'S GO BACK a long way in time. Around 800 BC, many things were happening, both good and bad. Legends (not necessarily reliable) make reference to coffee as far back as this. Homer and many Arabian stories tell of a beverage, black and bitter, with a mysterious power to stimulate. It has been suggested (although, I'm sure, many Scots will reject this) that whisky, first distilled in Asia, eventually found its way to Europe at this time via Egypt. Around this time we also get our earliest account of a chariot race. The winner would be rewarded with, among other things, 'a woman skilled in women's work'.

My history teachers taught me, rightly or wrongly, that somewhere around this time in Great Britain the Celts were battling the Anglo-Saxons. Having crossed the water into Kent, they continued right across southern England to Cornwall. They brought with them their language and, of course, their wonderful artistic talents. However, when the mighty Romans invaded later on, they had little effect on the Celts, although (working alongside the Saxons) they left England a pagan country. It was the Saxons who eventually almost wiped out the Celts, and Cornwall was one of the few places where the Celts kept Christianity alive. But what was happening in the Bible lands around this time?

It was around 800 BC that Ben-Hadad II was King of Syria and a guy called Naaman (whose name means 'pleasantness') was both one of his closest friends and one of his best commanders. This Naaman could not put a foot wrong. He had been promoted so high he was now on a par with the Syrian gods Rimmon, Baal and Ishtar! Probably even more important to his king was the fact that every time he went to war against Israel, he won! But … not everything was rosy for Naaman. His reputation, fortune and religion all failed to provide the one thing he needed most: a cure for his leprosy.

You see, in 800 BC lepers were viewed with fear and loathing. Dignitaries and officials who had once spent time with Naaman would now be avoiding him. Though mighty in battle, he was losing the fight against his decaying body. As a warrior, he would have preferred death by the sword to wasting away at the mercy of this dreadful disease. The symptoms he would have seen progressing would have included tiredness, pain in his joints and pus-filled lumps on his face. His eyebrows would fall out, his voice would fade and, as his nerves lost their feeling, discoloured patches would appear on his body. The prognosis? Eventually, his fingers, toes, hands and feet would lose all feeling, decay and drop off and finally his mind would go as well. Naaman would lose the will to live long before he lost his life.

In one of his battles with Israel, Naaman had captured a young girl whom he had dragged away from her family and friends to his own house. Her job there was to serve his wife as her slave. She heard, or maybe had even seen, that her master had this incurable skin disease. With all she had endured because of him, she could have been forgiven for thinking that it served him right. Maybe, even, that God was punishing him for making her an orphan in a strange land far from her home. But not so. Somehow she felt sorry for him. She advised Mrs Naaman that her husband should go and see a prophet, a man of God who lived in the city of Samaria near to where she used to live. She was confident he could heal him. With no other prospects of a cure, Mrs Naaman told her husband, who in turn told Ben-Hadad. The king didn't want to lose one of his best commanders to disease, so he decided to give this a try. It really was Naaman's last hope.

So, Ben-Hadad wrote a letter to Joram, the King of Israel, which went like this: 'Dear King Joram. Here is my commander Naaman. Cure his leprosy. I'll be sending some money and clothes over to you as a thank you for the miracle.' Now, Joram was the son of Ahab and Jezebel and he was pretty much as godless as his parents. It's not hard to see why he panicked as he read Ben-Hadad's letter.

'Who does he think I am?' he thought. 'I can't heal Naaman. Ben-Hadad just wants to pick a fight with me.'

Fortunately for him, Elisha, the man of God to whom the little girl was referring, heard about the crisis. He told Joram to calm down and send Naaman round to *his* house. He would show Naaman that there was a prophet of the one true God in Israel. So, Naaman was redirected and he and his small army arrived in all their splendour at Elisha's house. Here, the proud commander waited for the man of God to come out and lay hands on him and pray for his healing. Elisha did not appear. Instead, he sent someone out to give Naaman instructions on what to do. The man told Naaman that all he had to do was wash himself seven times in the River Jordan and then his leprosy would go.

The Syrian was furious! 'Where is this so-called man of God? He doesn't even have the courtesy to come out and talk to me! All he does is tell me to bathe in a horrible, smelly river! We have far cleaner rivers at home if I want a bath!' Naaman completely lost it. He jumped back in his chariot and raced off in a rage.

Eventually, his servants caught up with him. It took a brave man to approach him and ask him: 'Sir, if the man of God had asked you to do something dangerous that demanded courage, would you have done it?'

'Of course I would!' he retorted.

'Well, sir,' his servant continued, 'just think how easy it is to duck down in a river seven times.'

Eventually, Naaman humbled himself and went down to the Jordan. It truly was filthy and smelly. As he went under for the sixth time and came up stinking, you can imagine him glancing over menacingly at the man who had persuaded him to do it. On the seventh dip, however, his flesh became clean, just like it was when he was a baby! If I had been Naaman, I would probably have swum a couple of widths in sheer relief and happiness! He raced back to Elisha's house and thanked him. 'Now I know that there is no god in the entire world except the God of Israel.'

What can we learn from this wonderful story? Lots of things, really. God can do the impossible. Elisha was really in tune with God. Naaman had to be humble and obedient before he would get what he wanted. Sure, all valuable lessons. But, for me, the hero of the story is the little slave girl who had been dragged away from her friends and family and home. She still cared for the person who had taken her away from everyone and everything she loved.

When Jesus said, 'Love your enemies,' He really meant it. As Christians, we must not just love those who love us. Jesus' command is that we must love those who don't love us. Is that humanly possible? Probably not. But with God's help it can be done.

Say it again, Pete!

KEY VERSE 'I will always remind you of these things, even though you know them and are firmly established in the truth you now have.' 2 Peter 1:12 (NIV)

I WAS ONCE asked by a magazine: What makes you angry? My reply was, 'Nothing, really.' I explained that I rarely get cross, though I do sometimes get slightly annoyed over petty things, such as when people don't put their dirty dishes in the dishwasher. The principal culprits in my family (whose names I shall not disclose) have all read the article and are now in no doubt as to what annoys me, yet … they still don't put their dirty dishes in the machine. Not being one to give up, I have now bought a little plaque that hangs above the dishwasher to provide a gentle reminder. It simply states: 'You don't need a degree to load the dishwasher.' Subtle and, of course, not aimed at any particular individual; but sadly even that is proving to be totally ineffective.

In our reading today, Peter makes no apology about sending out reminders and repeating himself. We all need to be reminded about things. The trouble is, it seems the older I get the more I need to be reminded and the more I seem to keep repeating myself! One of my friends decided to move from a lively, non-traditional church to his local, traditional parish church. He enjoyed the services but he had problems with the liturgy, because to him liturgy just seemed to be 'vain repetition'. He failed to see that the strength of the liturgy is that it is repetition but far from vain. Someone has defined it as follows:

> 'Constant repetition helps to free the worshipper from the actual words of the liturgy. They become familiar with the words, and are then able to focus on the meaning of the words. This then leads to a personalising of that meaning. Each element of the liturgy can then be used as a platform from which to personally approach Christ in unison with their fellow believers.'

When I was in hospital enjoying heavy doses of chemotherapy and morphine, I discovered that my brain couldn't cope with free prayer but it did understand liturgy, mainly because what was being said was repetitive and familiar to me.

By being repetitive, Peter was trying to stir up his readers to remember the truths of Christianity. False teaching was a constant threat to this newly formed church and he believed that the best way to avoid being taken in by heresy was continually to remember what the truth is. When he used the words 'I will make every effort' in 2 Peter 1:15, he meant 'to stir them up'. This is strong, urgent stuff because the word literally means 'wake' or 'rouse' and is the same word that is used in relation to a storm on the Sea of Galilee.

God knows that as human beings we need constant reminders. We read in Scripture that He didn't want the Jewish nation ever to forget certain important events in their history, so He ordained particular annual festivals and feast days to jog their memory. I believe that as Christians the best way for us to stay strong in our faith is to be continually reminded of Jesus. One way that can help us to do this is following the events of the liturgical or church year, as many do. Celebrating Advent, Christmas, Lent, Easter, Ascension and Pentecost and so on at specific times of the year reminds us constantly of the biblical events surrounding the life of Jesus. As we repeat this cycle each year, our memory is continually refreshed. The ultimate constant reminder for the believer is, of course, taking part in the Eucharist. Jesus Himself said of the bread and the wine: 'This is My body and blood given for you. Do this in remembrance of Me.'

As I have said, 2 Peter was written to counteract the beliefs and activities of false teachers, who were a threat to the Church. The reason Peter was being even more diligent than usual in reinforcing certain points was that he knew that the time left to him on earth was short. But he was in a frustrating position. He was imprisoned hundreds of miles away from the Christians he wanted to remind. In those days, news travelled slowly and it took a long time for him to hear of things going wrong – just as it took a long time to send his words of advice back. In what was to prove his last message, he wanted to underline the importance of knowing God and growing in Him. That, of course, is a message that can't be repeated too many times.

Here we get a wonderful glimpse of Peter the pastor. In John 21, we find him with the resurrected Jesus by the Sea of Galilee, where His Lord tells him three times to tend His flock. Jesus was saying that He wanted the 'fisher of men' to become a shepherd, and in today's reading we can see how those few words from Him changed His disciple's life.

We can see that right to the end Peter was concerned for his 'flock' and determined to ensure that it would be safe and nurtured. He even wanted to arrange for its care after he had gone. Peter knew something that I don't know and actually am rather glad I don't know. Jesus had revealed to him how and when he would die. He had been told that it would not be until he was old.

This may explain why, in a prison cell in Jerusalem, the night before he was due to be executed on King Herod's orders, Peter managed to sleep like a baby. He knew that his life was not going to end that way. It was safe until his work on this earth was completed. We can see that Peter had no fear of death. He almost seemed to be looking forward to his eventual departure.

What a wonderful word 'departure' is! For believers, death is like leaving an airport departure lounge to fly to a far better place. Our human bodies, like Peter's, are temporal, made just for our time on earth. Death is a walk through a door into the real life of eternity. We needn't approach it with fear, because that is a fear Jesus overcame – in practice, not just in theory. But while we remain in our temporal bodies, let's heed Peter's final reminder and seek to know Jesus ever better and keep growing closer to Him.

Or, to quote the old spiritual song that has served as a reminder to believers for over a hundred years:

'Just a closer walk with Thee,
Grant it, Jesus, is my plea,
Daily walking close to Thee,
Let it be, dear Lord, let it be.'

Thank God for reminders!

❯ Holy Moses!

KEY VERSE

'He wraps you in goodness – beauty eternal.
He renews your youth – you're always young in
his presence.' Psalm 103:5 (The Message)

LIVING TODAY, IT'S quite hard to imagine how life must have been back in Old Testament times. I want us to travel back approximately 3,300 years to meet an eighty-year-old man. Most eighty-year-olds today would be thinking that their best years were way behind them, and I dare say this guy had been thinking similar thoughts as he settled down into a nice, easy (but very boring) way of life.

The person we are talking about is Moses. He spent his time wandering around and, no doubt, like most older people, reminiscing about the good old days he'd had when he was younger. It's very easy, when considering your past, to do so with rose-tinted spectacles and remember only the good times! You see, Moses had spent his childhood and youth having fun and adventures (and, of course, the odd tricky moment) living as a prince in Egypt. But now that was all ancient history. These days, he was much older and far more mature and had settled down with a wife and son. The principal excitement in his life was making sure that his father-in-law's sheep had enough to eat.

One day, searching for more grass, Moses found himself climbing up a 7,500-foot mountain and it was there that he saw something strange: a bush that was on fire. Well, actually, at first glance what he saw was not so strange – in fact, it must have been quite commonplace. It seems that for bushes to ignite spontaneously is not so unusual in this area; but what made this particular conflagration different was that the leaves and branches kept burning and burning but were not being charred or consumed. That *is* very unusual.

For Moses, it was certainly worth wandering away from the sheep to take a closer look. This was God's way of grabbing his attention, because as he approached the burning bush he heard a voice call his name twice. He replied, 'Here I am' – although the voice seemed to be coming from inside the bush! I can imagine him peering around trying to spot the person who was calling him. There was no one in sight, but the voice from inside the bush told him not to come any closer because he was walking on holy ground and to take his shoes off. Moses would have been wearing shoes made of leather, wood or matted grass. I guess that he immediately did what the talking bush told him to do. It was time for the ex-prince of Egypt to humble himself.

Now, we must remember that it wasn't the bush or the ground that was holy, it was God's presence. Some people today treat certain buildings as holy, but they are not holy in themselves. What makes somewhere holy is the presence in that place either of God or of people who have had an encounter with Him – like Jacob in Genesis 28.

It was at this point that God introduced Himself. It was no longer a burning bush talking but almighty God Himself. 'I am the God of your fathers, of Abraham, Isaac and Jacob.' Moses hid his face, understandably frightened to look at God. Once his sandals were off and his face hidden, God gave him his commission for the next forty years. He was now being told the reason he had been born.

We have all travelled different routes and experienced different things to get where we are today. Nothing is by chance or wasted. We can learn lessons from everything we have done. Moses had learned to live as a prince and knew the palace protocol, which would be a great help later when he eventually approached Pharaoh. It would have been impossible for him to get an audience with such an exalted person if he had just shown up as a nomadic shepherd and knocked on the palace door. But he had also learned to live as a nomadic shepherd. Not only did he know how to look after sheep but he had also been hardened to survive out in the wilds, walking long distances and living on very little. This was going to prove invaluable in his forthcoming forty years of wandering in the wilderness.

The thing that really stands out for me in this story is that Moses never really found his purpose in life until he learned reverence and humility. For me personally, being humble is a constant learning process, not a thing that I could master in one go. Reverence, however, is something that I did learn quickly. For most of my life, I had been encouraged to treat God informally and consider Jesus my best friend. Looking back, I'm sure I didn't always give Him the respect and reverence He deserves. Certainly, I remember that when I first went to a Communion service in Chichester Cathedral I found it very quiet and formal and yet somehow very precious. I experienced a different sense of the presence of God than I had previously known.

Now, of course I'm not saying that my informality with God was wrong, but I knew that for me personally the time had come when I needed to show God more respect and reverence. An old word that has crept into some of our modern praise songs is 'awe'. According to Wikipedia, this word denotes a feeling comparable to wonder but less joyous and more fearful. I needed a bit more awe in my life. I needed to take off my shoes and hide my face. Since then, I have to admit, new avenues of ministry have opened up, for which I am so grateful to God.

I used to think that the older I got the less God would be able to use me. I would no longer have the energy to do the God-inspired things I used to do when I was younger. Over the past few years, I've discovered (in all humility) that that is not the case. So, unless God specifically tells us to settle down and look after sheep, we must always be ready to move on to the next adventure He has lined up for us, however old we are. Even if we are over eighty!

God plays His joker!

'Men and women look at the face; GOD looks into the heart.' 1 Samuel 16:7 (The Message)

KEY VERSE

WHEN I FIRST became a true believer, around the age of twenty, I loved music and hoped that God might one day use me in that field. One day, I was invited to audition at a very early 'Christian's Got Talent' event at Portsmouth Guildhall. Standing alone on the large stage, I sang my song. When I was finished, the judge looked up at me from the front row of the auditorium and called out that my performance might have sounded better if my guitar had been in tune. I retorted that I thought it was in tune. Well, it seemed to be in tune with my voice – but maybe that was out of tune as well!

I realise now that in many ways I am God's joke. I have probably released more albums than anyone else on the Christian circuit, and yet despite a lifetime of practice I am still not what anyone would describe as a tuneful singer – and I still can't tune a guitar! I often think that electronic guitar tuners were invented just for me.

Men and women look at the face; GOD looks into the heart. In the days I worked with children, I was always on the lookout to see whether any of them had a special gift or talent that later might be used to the glory of God. Many years ago, I was about to perform in one venue when a young lad refused to get off the stage. I went up to him and he told me he was going to sing with Ishmael that night. I looked at him and saw nothing special. In fact, if anything he seemed a little over-confident. I told him gently that I was Ishmael and he should go back to his seat as I was singing that night, not him. Years later, that same guy approached me and reminded me of that occasion. Since then, he had had three number-one chart singles and sold many millions of albums. His name is Daniel Bedingfield. Nowadays? Yes Daniel, you can sing on stage with me any time you like!

Men and women look at the face; GOD looks into the heart. The prophet Samuel was sent by God to find a future king from the sons of Jesse. Samuel was still looking at the outward appearance. A while earlier, he had anointed a very tall, strong, good-looking man called Saul, and now he was looking for someone similarly endowed to be his successor. It made sense – every army would like a giant of a man at its head. Of course, a short while later David would discover that Goliath was a great hit with the Philistine army but he would be an even greater hit with his pebble. So, seven sons of Jesse were paraded before Samuel, no doubt standing tall and sticking out their chests. Samuel was impressed – but God was not. He was looking at their hearts. After a while, the neglected youngest boy of the family was brought in, like an afterthought. His physique may not quite have matched his brothers, but David the shepherd boy had just the heart God was looking for.

Later, we read that David had many attributes that must have pleased God. He was patient, loyal, full of faith and wisdom, full of zeal, a fearless leader – and so we could go on. But I just want to mention three things we can learn from David if we, too, want hearts that are pleasing to God.

First, David knew how to worship God. He may have been a brilliant singer, songwriter, musician, but that doesn't necessarily make you a true worshipper. But David knew that worship must come from the heart. Only when that was right with God could he truly express his praise and worship through his musicianship and his God-given creativity. If his heart had not been consistently trying to please God, his psalms would have ended up no more than interesting poems, not God-inspired hymns.

Then, David knew how to be honest with God. Only close friends can be totally honest with each other without either of them being hurt or offended, and as we read about David we see that he was one of God's close friends. Over the past few years, I have questioned God many times and wondered where He was when I needed Him most. It has shocked some of my Christian friends that I should ask God why He wasn't listening to me or answering my prayers. But listen to these scriptures as rendered by *The Message*, because this is how David may have expressed himself today:

'GOD, are you avoiding me?
Where are you when I need you?'
(Psalm 10:1)

'God, God … my God!
Why did you dump me
miles from nowhere?

Doubled up with pain, I call to God
all the day long. No answer. Nothing.'
(Psalm 22:1–2)

'Get up, GOD! Are you going to sleep all day?
Wake up! Don't you care what happens to us?
Why do you bury your face in the pillow?
Why pretend things are just fine with us?
And here we are – flat on our faces in the dirt,
held down with a boot on our necks,
Get up and come to our rescue.
If you love us so much, *Help us!*'
(Psalm 44:23–26)

These scriptures seem downright disrespectful to God, yet they are a genuine representation of how the psalmist was feeling. I have learned from David that if I'm not honest with God, I am actually insulting Him. God sees my heart and if my prayer is not saying what my heart is feeling, it really is no prayer at all.

And, of course, David knew how to repent before God. He was far from perfect and committed some dreadful sins, but he was willing to face up to them and plead to God to forgive him. Just as he had spoken honestly to his friend God, so God spoke honestly to David when he let Him down. David confessed his sins and took the consequences.

Now is an ideal time for us to be honest with God. I believe that God doesn't want us to spend most of our lives examining ourselves and seeing how bad we are. I think He would rather we spent more time examining Jesus and seeing how good He is. The more we look at Jesus, the more the Holy Spirit will reveal to us our weaknesses and failings so that we can face them head-on and ask for God's forgiveness. Unlike David, we know that Jesus died so that our sins can be forgiven and forgotten. Through repentance and confession, we can be made clean and can start afresh. According to 1 John 1:9 (*The Message*): 'If we admit our sins – make a clean breast of them – he won't let us down; he'll be true to himself. He'll forgive our sins and purge us of all wrongdoing.'

Sadly, other people often still choose to look at our outward appearance – and usually at our faults, not our good points. But today's good news is that, whatever men and women look at, God is still far more interested in looking at our hearts.

A little poem for you:

My sins are clear for all to see,
They have been from the start;
But God ignores the outward me
If He sees a faithful heart.

Prophet and loss

KEY VERSE

'Peter and the apostles answered, "It's necessary to obey God rather than men."' Acts 5:29 (The Message)

WHAT I AM going to retell to you, I consider to be one of the strangest stories in the Bible.

Before his death, Solomon puts a guy called Jeroboam in charge of his building operations in Ephraim. All seems to be going fairly well until Jeroboam is approached by the prophet Ahijah, who happens to be wearing a new cloak. As Jeroboam watches, Ahijah takes off this cloak and tears it into twelve pieces. He then tells Jeroboam to take ten of the pieces for himself, as the Lord is saying that he is going to be ruler over ten tribes of Israel. God is going to take most of the kingdom away from Solomon's heir because the people have forsaken Him and are worshipping other gods. However, because He loves David and the city of Jerusalem, He will allow Solomon's heir to rule there. When Solomon hears about this, he tries to kill Jeroboam; but he flees to Egypt, where he is given political asylum.

As soon as Jeroboam hears that Solomon has died, he returns home – just as one of Solomon's sons, Rehoboam, is about to be anointed king. Jeroboam and 'the whole assembly of Israel' approach Rehoboam and tell him that his father put a heavy yoke on them, by levying excessive taxes and conscripting labour, but if he will lighten that yoke, they will all serve him. Rehoboam asks for three days to think this through. When he consults his father's advisers, they say that he should lighten the people's burden; but when he turns to the friends with whom he has grown up, they say the opposite. In fact, they actually urge him to say: 'My father scourged you with whips; I will scourge you with scorpions!' Foolishly, Rehoboam decides to take his friends' advice. When Jeroboam and the assembly hear his reply, it is the last straw. The prophecy of Ahijah is fulfilled as the Kingdom of Israel splits from Judah and, very soon afterwards, Jeroboam is anointed as its first king, leaving Rehoboam just with Judah. The great realm of David and Solomon has been broken up into two smaller, quarrelling states.

Things do not go well for either of the new kings. Rehoboam wants to go to war against Israel to get back his whole kingdom, but God instructs His people not to fight against their brothers. Rehoboam will have to be content with what he has. Jeroboam has a very different issue to deal with. If the people of Israel keep going up to Jerusalem to worship God there, there is a very good chance that eventually they will change their allegiance and start serving the King of Judah. Of course, that would mean death for Jeroboam. He has to think of a way to keep his kingdom together.

After taking advice, he decides to tell his people that it is much too far to keep going up to Jerusalem to worship God and so he has created his own gods for them to worship. He has altars built and golden calves installed at Bethel and Dan, and places shrines on various high places. He even appoints priests (not Levites). Soon, the people of Israel are cheerfully worshipping Jeroboam's new gods. Understandably, God is not happy with this scheme.

One day, as Jeroboam is standing by one of the altars in Bethel, a young prophet arrives and utters these amazing words:

'In years to come, a son named Josiah will come and sacrifice your priests on these very altars. A sign that I am telling the truth is that this altar will split apart and the ashes will fall everywhere.'

Now, what makes this so amazing is that he prophesied this 300 years before Josiah was even born and he not only predicted correctly what would happen but he even got Josiah's name right! Jeroboam is furious. This is not what he wants to hear, and it certainly is not something he wants his people to hear! 'Seize him!' he cries to his men, pointing at the young prophet, but even as he does so, his hand shrivels up. And, as he stares at it in disbelief, the altar splits in half and the ashes go everywhere.

Jeroboam is in a terrible state. He begs the young prophet to pray for him that his hand might be restored – though not that he might change his ways. God duly heals him. Naturally, the king is delighted to have the use of his hand back and he invites the young prophet to come home with him for a meal and a gift. The prophet replies that even if Jeroboam were to give him half his possessions he wouldn't go back with him. He will not eat or drink in Bethel, as God has specifically told him not to. He even has instructions not to go back to his own home by the route he came.

Now, there is an old prophet living in Bethel and when he hears what has happened, he has his donkey saddled up and he goes looking for the young prophet. He finds him sitting under a tree and invites him to come home with him for a meal. The young man gives him the same answer he gave the king: that he must not eat or drink in Bethel or go home the way he came. The old man tells him that he, too, is a prophet and an angel has told him that the situation has changed and it is now all right for the young man to come back with him. Which is a lie. So, the young prophet goes back with him for a meal. While they are eating, a genuine word from the Lord comes to the old man and he prophesies that because the young man has disobeyed God, his body will not be buried with his ancestors. The Bible doesn't tell us how the young man reacts to this revelation!

After the meal, the old prophet saddles his own donkey for the young man and sends him on his way; but he hasn't gone far before a lion attacks him and kills him. Some passers-by see his body lying in the road with both the lion and the donkey just standing beside it. They go and tell the old prophet, who finds another donkey and hastens off to check this out for himself. He is amazed to see that the lion has neither eaten the body nor mauled the donkey. It's as if they are both standing guard waiting for him to arrive. The old man takes the body home and buries it in his own tomb. He mourns for the young prophet and gives instructions that eventually he himself should be buried alongside him.

You must admit that this is a very strange little story; but we can still learn something from it. I'm guessing that the young prophet was tired, hungry and thirsty when the old prophet found him resting under a tree. He would have had a natural respect for the older man, especially as he claimed to have had a supernatural experience and met an angel. And, let's face it, unlike the king, this old prophet was only offering him a meal, not a reward. It could so easily be God intervening to refresh him.

However, when you are given a direct word from God you must act on it and not allow yourself to be diverted by an alternative proposal, however tempting it might be. Although we listen to other believers, we have the Holy Spirit dwelling in us and God speaks to us personally. Older and more mature believers have a responsibility to encourage those younger than them to obey the will of the Lord for their lives. But sometimes even well-meant words of guidance can mislead or even manipulate others and cause them to lose their way. This is sin. When God tells any of us to do something, let's get on and do it! It's highly unlikely that He is going to change His mind.

Insured but not fully protected

'I do not ask that You will take them out of the world, but that You will keep and *protect them from the evil one.' John 17:15 (Amplified Bible)*

HERE WE FIND Jesus asking God for protection for His followers. But what sort of protection is He asking for? I think that one or two of us get slightly confused. Wouldn't it be great if Jesus were asking God to protect His followers from all illness and infirmity? The so-called Faith Movement believes that we needn't suffer illness. They quote Isaiah 53:5, 'By his wounds we are healed', in support of this claim. In his wonderful book *God on Mute*, Pete Greig tells of a friend who had made the 'faith-healing tele-evangelists' his role models. He told Pete that God had miraculously healed his back pain. He added that it was just the symptoms that he couldn't seem to get rid of.

When I was diagnosed with leukaemia, some people advised me not to have chemotherapy, as that would be showing lack of faith. I was reminded that 'by Jesus' wounds I had been healed' – I just had to believe that and claim my healing! I never felt I was lacking in faith, I just praised God for doctors and medicine.

If the 'faith boys' are right, why didn't sick Christians 'claim their healing' in New Testament times? Trophimus was sick. Epaphroditus fell ill and almost died. Paul himself implies in Galatians 4 that he had a nasty eye problem that incapacitated him, and in 2 Corinthians 12 refers to a strange 'thorn in his flesh' that kept him humble. Unlike some, I'm not convinced he was referring to his wife! So, I guess Jesus wasn't asking God to protect His followers from illness or infirmity.

Wouldn't it be great if Jesus were asking God to protect His followers from all violence? I was shocked, back in March 1986, when I first heard about a gang of burglars breaking into Ealing Vicarage. The vicar, Michael Saward, was beaten up and his daughter raped. If Jesus was asking God to protect His followers from violence, where was He that lunchtime?

When I visited Rome, I was impressed by St Peter's and the Sistine Chapel but what really affected me more than anything was seeing the Catacombs. Just the one we visited was the final resting place of half a million believers – young and old, martyred just for following Jesus. The martyr we were told about who has remained most in my memory was a fourteen-year-old Christian girl who was tortured for three days and finally beheaded. The emperors responsible for these atrocities nearly 2,000 years ago were Nero and Domitian. They caused immense suffering for the Early Church.

Diocletian's cruelty towards Christians 250 years later was even worse. During those three centuries, I wonder whether any of the believers questioned where the protection Jesus had asked for had got to. I think that, like Paul, they considered it an honour and a privilege to suffer for Him, just as He had suffered for them. So, I guess Jesus wasn't asking God to protect His followers from violence.

Wouldn't it be great if Jesus were asking God to protect His followers from a painful death? When I was seven years old, I heard about Jim Elliot and four other missionaries who were speared in the Ecuadorian jungle by Auca Indians. Even as a child, I wondered why Jesus did not protect His missionaries. Why did He allow them to suffer such a horrific death? Later on, I heard that Jim's wife, Elisabeth, and his daughter, Valerie, not only forgave his murderers but continued working among the Auca people. Not surprisingly, many became Christians. Even today, we know that many of our brothers and sisters in other countries are being persecuted and martyred for their faith. So, I guess Jesus wasn't asking God to protect His followers from a painful death.

So, what exactly was Jesus asking His Father to protect His followers from? A line from the Lord's Prayer that Jesus repeats in John 17 contains the answer: 'Deliver us' not from evil but 'from the evil one.' Jesus emphasised that His followers no longer belong to this world. God's enemy is now also our enemy. Peter tells us that 'the devil prowls around like a roaring lion looking for someone to devour' (1 Pet. 5:8).

We certainly need God's protection – protection from the evil one himself. Jesus said: 'My prayer is not to take them out of the world.' It seems that those who follow Jesus will not be exempt from illness, violence or a painful death. What Jesus was implying is a paradox. Where we are safest – where God's protection is guaranteed – is among those who could hurt us most. Our commission, like the apostles', is to share the love and good news of Jesus with those who at present live in the dark because they have been blinded by the prince of darkness.

This is where Christians will find spiritual protection, although (as martyrs throughout history have proven) rarely physical protection. When the evil one throws all kinds of hardship and tribulation at us, Jesus asks God to protect us and help us stay strong in our faith until the very end. Like many Bible heroes in difficult times, we all question God. We may even ask: How *can* God protect us? What does He, high up in heaven, know about suffering, pain and death? To answer that, let me finish with an anonymous story I first heard in the 1970s and have never forgotten. You may have heard it before, but it's certainly worth hearing again.

THE LONG SILENCE
At the end of time, billions of people were scattered on a great plain before God's throne. Most shrank back from the brilliant light before them, but some groups near the front talked heatedly – not with cringing shame but with belligerence.

'Can God judge us? How can He know about suffering?' snapped a pert young brunette. She ripped open a sleeve to reveal a tattooed number from a Nazi concentration camp. 'We endured terror, beatings, torture, death!'

In another group, an African-American boy lowered his collar. 'What about this?' he demanded, showing an ugly rope burn. 'Lynched – for no crime but being black!'

In another crowd, a pregnant schoolgirl with sullen eyes. 'Why should I suffer?' she murmured. 'It wasn't my fault.'

Far across the plain there were hundreds of such groups. Each had a complaint against God for the evil and suffering He had permitted in His world.

How lucky God was to live in Heaven, where all was sweetness and light. Where there was no weeping or fear, no hunger or hatred. What did God know of all that man had been forced to endure in this world? For God leads a pretty sheltered life, they said.

So, each of these groups sent forth their leader, chosen because he had suffered the most. A Jew, an African-American, a person from Hiroshima, a horribly deformed arthritic, a thalidomide child. In the centre of the vast plain they consulted with each other. At last they were ready to present their case. It was rather clever.

Before God could be qualified to be their judge, He must endure what they had endured.

Their decision was that God should be sentenced to live on earth as a man.

Let Him be born a Jew.

Let the legitimacy of His birth be doubted.

Give Him a work so difficult that even His family will think Him out of His mind.

Let Him be betrayed by His closest friends.

Let Him face false charges, be tried by a prejudiced jury and convicted by a cowardly judge.

Let Him be tortured.

At the last, let Him see what it means to be terribly alone. Then let Him die.

Let Him die so there can be no doubt He died. Let there be a great host of witnesses to verify it.

As each leader pronounced His portion of the sentence, loud murmurs of approval went up from the throng of people assembled.

But when the last had finished pronouncing sentence, there was a long silence.

No one uttered a word. No one moved. For suddenly all knew that God had already served His sentence.

I'm in with the in crowd

KEY VERSE

'You are My friends if you keep on doing the things which I command you to do.' John 15:14 (Amplified Bible)

I'M SURE SOME of you suffered like I did in the games lesson at school. I was pretty good at football – at least, I thought I was. But when it was time to pick teams, the games teacher always chose his two favourite pupils as captains. The rest of us would stand in a long line facing them as they made their selections. First the captains would choose their best friends, and then the best players. Then they would pick the bullies (because they were scared that if they didn't, they'd get a hiding later). After the fittest came the fattest. The large boys would look sturdy in defence and so on … Until finally there were only two boys left. Yep, yours truly and one other boy – usually someone who hated football and would much rather have sat on the grass at the side of the pitch and made daisy chains.

A while ago, while studying the story of Jonah, I decided I wanted to look at the subject of favourites. Has God got favourites? Maybe 'favourite' is the wrong word to use with regard to the Old Testament, when God seems to have chosen certain people to do certain tasks. We are left in no doubt that Israel was then God's chosen nation – but was it the only nation He showed favour towards?

Actually, it seems not. It's obvious that He was reaching out to many other, pagan nations as well. He sent some of His best prophets to urge them to repent. Obadiah was sent to Edom. Nahum preached in Assyria. Zephaniah prophesied to Canaan and Ethiopia. Amos and Ezekiel delivered judgments to the Ammonites, the Phoenicians, the Egyptians and the Edomites. As for Jonah, God sent him to the people of Nineveh in Assyria. God cared for these nations even though – like Israel – they were all far from perfect.

So, we can see that God wanted a relationship with other nations; but what about individuals? The Old Testament mentions that God had special friends – Abraham, Moses and David were undoubtedly three of them. But He also chose some very unlikely Gentiles as friends. Four women come to mind whom many (including the ancient Jewish author of the *Book of Jubilees*) regard as non-Jews. To us, they might seem rather unlikely candidates for friendship with God. Tamar the Aramean disguised herself as a prostitute, and Rahab the Caananite *was* one. Bathsheba was married to a Hittite and got drawn into adultery. And then there was Ruth the Moabite, who married Boaz, a Jew – even though God didn't seem very happy about Jews marrying Moabites. What makes these four even more special is that (as we read in Matthew 1) God chose them to be ancestors of Jesus. Even though, once again, they were all far from perfect.

On to the New Testament. Did Jesus have favourites? He was certainly very close to Mary, Martha and Lazarus, Mary Magdalene and, of course, His mother, Mary. He also was very close to at least eleven of His disciples, and especially to three of them: Peter, James and John. And in John's Gospel we are told of one particular disciple 'whom Jesus loved'. His identity is never actually revealed, but most commentators assume it was John! Jesus was close friends with these individuals even though they were all far from perfect.

And so to today. Does God still have friends, favourites and chosen ones? Although He wants everyone on the planet to be His friend, we know that, sadly, not everyone wishes to be – and He will never force His friendship on anyone. I do believe that God still calls people and still has specific tasks for each of His friends to fulfil. However, our free will allows us to choose to accept that call and fulfil that task – or choose not to.

This brings up the controversial question: Are the Jews still God's chosen people? The debate continues. Say yes and then God must be heartbroken because still, after two thousand years, the vast majority of them still reject His Son as their Messiah. Say no and you will be accused of believing in a replacement theology. (Which says that, because the Jews have failed in their God-given task, He has replaced them with the Church.) It's all a bit confusing because Paul, who is a leading authority, tells us in Romans 11 that God has not cast away His people and they are still the apple of His eye but in Galatians 3 tells us that now there is neither Jew nor Greek as we are all one in Christ Jesus. As I say, the debate continues! Maybe the Jews are still God's chosen people, but maybe so, too, are the Gentiles.

So, what makes someone a friend of God today? A true friend of God is someone who realises that they are a hopeless sinner who needs to repent and that Jesus is the perfect Saviour. A true friend of God is someone whose aim is to put God first in their life and who does their best to love those around them as much as they love themselves. A true friend of God is someone who has a heart that wants to do the things God asks them to do – even if they don't always manage it! The best news ever is that God wants us all as His friends, even though we are all far from perfect.

Finally, will God have favourites in heaven? Well, I don't know. But one thing I do know. Maybe one day when I've left this earth I will be standing in a seemingly never-ending line of countless millions. Every person's name is being read out from the Lamb's Book of Life. Maybe I will hear your name read out long before mine. Maybe I will be left right until last – apart from one other person standing next to me.

Zacchaeus. Why Zacchaeus? Well, perhaps because the names were read out in alphabetical order. Perhaps because the shortest people were asked to stand at the end of the queue. Or perhaps, most likely, because he and I were both pretty bad lads while on earth. Would I feel rejected being left until last, like I did back in my old school football days? Definitely not! I would just be so thankful for God's grace and mercy and so relieved that, even though I have done nothing to deserve it, He has kept me as one of His friends until the very end. Even though I have lived a life that was far from perfect!

The disabled carer

KEY VERSE

'The king asked, "Is there anyone left from the family of Saul to whom I can show some godly kindness?" Ziba told the king, "Yes, there is Jonathan's son, lame in both feet."' 2 Samuel 9:3 (The Message)

THE BIBLE IS full of stories about heroes and villains, the young and the old, the healthy and the sick; but there are very few Bible characters who have disabilities.

Although my hearing had begun to deteriorate after I reached sixty – probably due to a lifetime of loud music – I was given an antibiotic called Gentamicin on my first night in hospital after being diagnosed with leukaemia and I don't think it has helped my hearing. After extensive treatment, I was examined by a Harley Street consultant, who said that it isn't just my hearing, I also have a problem with 'speech indiscrimination'. In other words, even if I can hear what you're saying, sometimes my brain has trouble deciphering it. But I'm not complaining. Those medications helped to keep me alive, and I'd rather be alive with a hearing disability than dead! It is strange, though, that people never feel embarrassed making jokes about my deafness, usually saying 'Pardon?' when I mention it. If I was partially blind, I'm not sure that anyone would dare make jokes about that!

A while ago, I was invited to go skiing with my daughter and son-in-law. The last and only time I had attempted to ski was fifteen years earlier. Being over sixty, I knew deep down that I was too old to learn; but being over sixty, I also was never going to admit to that fact! The first day on the piste, as we approached a rather steep S-bend, my companions were amazed to see me fly past them. They thought I was skiing brilliantly! Little did they realise that I just didn't know how to stop. On the next bend, I flew straight into a snowdrift, fell over, and felt a nasty tear in the back of the calf muscle on my left leg. Needless to say, that was the end of my skiing career. For the rest of the week, I was limping around the resort in agony.

Way back in the tenth century BC, we read that one of King Saul's grandsons had a serious disability. Mephibosheth was only five years old when his father, Jonathan, and grandfather, Saul, were killed in battle on Mount Gilboa. On hearing the news, he fled with his nurse but in the rush he fell and became crippled. When David eventually became king, he enquired whether any of Saul's family was still alive.

In those days, when a new king asked such a question it was usually because he wanted to kill off his predecessor's remaining relatives; but not so with Mephibosheth. Not only did David spare his life, he also moved him into the royal palace and gave him all of Saul's personal possessions. Mephibosheth was overcome by David's generosity, and Ziba (who had formerly been Saul's servant) now became Mephibosheth's. David treated him as one of his own sons.

Nonetheless, having a disability of any sort does make life more difficult and at times it can make you feel quite down and even depressed, and this was certainly so with Mephibosheth. Not being able to walk like everyone else seemed to give him very low self-worth – he even referred to himself on one occasion as 'a dead dog'.

One day, David's son Absalom revolted against his father. Soon, his forces were poised to take Jerusalem. David decided to make a run for it with his entire household. After they had travelled a short distance, Ziba approached him with donkeys loaded with provisions and explained that these were gifts for him to sustain him on his journey. David then asked the obvious question: Where was his master, Mephibosheth?

Ziba told David that he was staying in Jerusalem, hoping that Israel would give him back his grandfather's kingdom. Which, of course, implied that he was in cahoots with Absalom. It's hard to work out whether David was angry, sad or both when he heard this but, however he felt, he told Ziba that from that moment on he could have everything that belonged to Mephibosheth. Ziba seemed delighted.

Some time later, Absalom was defeated and David returned to Jerusalem. Mephibosheth went to meet him. We read that he had really let himself go. He hadn't taken care of his feet, trimmed his moustache or washed his clothes since the day the king fled the city. He seemed genuinely pleased to see David's safe return. David asked him: Why didn't you come with me? Mephibosheth gave his reasons and claimed that Ziba had betrayed him and slandered him. He then honoured David and thanked him for all the love and kindness he had shown him in the past even though he did not deserve it. David told him not to say any more. Obviously, he had more important things to do than to get involved in a dispute between Mephibosheth and Ziba. He just said that they should divide the property in question between the two of them.

We have to ask ourselves, though: Why would a warrior like David, with so much blood on his hands, be kind to Mephibosheth? Well, we know that David always showed loyalty to the previous king, whom God had chosen and the prophet Samuel had anointed. We know, too, that he had made a vow to Jonathan before the Lord and would always have wanted to show kindness to his best friend's family. That said, other members of Saul's family had suffered badly. David had allowed the Gibeonites to kill seven of them in retaliation for things Saul had done. And David didn't have to be loyal to Saul, who had been his worst enemy – and nobody else even knew about his vow to Jonathan except God.

I must admit that, based on what the Bible tells us, I'm not a great fan of Ziba. He was obviously creeping up to David in giving him the laden donkeys and telling lies about Mephibosheth because he wanted David to give him Saul's goods. Mephibosheth, on the other hand, I do have a bit of time for. He'd lost his dad at an early age, he'd lived most of his life with a serious disability (at a time when he wouldn't get any sympathy for it but only mockery) – and he seems to have coped pretty well. I also reckon he truly was very appreciative of David. If he really had thrown in his lot with Absalom in the hope that he could claim the throne, surely he would not have let his appearance get so out of hand?

But the thing that clinches it for me is that when David told him and Ziba to divide Saul's property between them, he wasn't interested in material things and said that Ziba could keep the lot. He was just pleased that David had arrived back safe and sound. That's why I believe that Mephibosheth the disabled man was also Mephibosheth the carer. He cared for David.

Without meaning to sound in any way patronising, being slightly disabled myself, could I ask you to be thoughtful towards people with disabilities? We don't want extra-special attention; we just want to be treated the same as everyone else as we offer to God what we are able to do, along with the rest of His people.

Nic, not too quick but a solid brick!

KEY VERSE *'That's salvation. With your whole being you embrace God setting things right, and then you say it, right out loud: "God has set everything right between him and me!"' Romans 10:9 (The Message)*

IN THE DAYS of Jesus, the Pharisees were a minority group of middle- and upper-class Jews numbering about six thousand. The word 'Pharisee' means 'holy one'. They had worked out that the Law contained 613 commandments, 248 positive and 365 negative – and all to be obeyed. But, for them, that wasn't enough laws, so they came up with even more to elaborate on the 613. For instance, the Sabbath law now had 39 subsections. Tying a knot in a rope on the Sabbath counted as work, but if you could do it with one hand, that was legal. It was OK to tie a knot in a woman's belt, so you could use a woman's belt to haul a bucket of water up from a well on the Sabbath, but not a rope. For Pharisees, keeping these rules was almost a matter of life and death.

But there were still more laws, oral as well as written down. Laws relating to fasting, washing, the preparation of food and so on. The Pharisees were generally not violent, although they hated Rome, but they did have a political wing called the Zealots. One of Jesus' disciples, Simon, was an ex-Zealot. The Pharisees had a reputation for being the 'people's party' that seemed to have little love or respect for the common people. Their self-appointed role was to try and make sure that every Jew obeyed all the laws to the letter.

Quite distinct from them were the teachers of the Law (or 'scribes'). They spent their lives poring over the Law of Moses, so they knew a lot about it. To become a 'scribe', you had to complete a 26-year course, starting at the age of fourteen. Once you had qualified, you might even join the Sanhedrin. Their concern was to see that nobody tried to change the Law. The 'scribes' came up with the extra laws that the Pharisees then policed.

The Sadducees were different again. They were an upper-class religious/political party. Sadducees held top jobs in the Temple and the Jewish state and were made rich by bribery. They didn't believe in any afterlife, unlike the Pharisees, who hated them because they were happy to do deals with Rome. And the written Law was enough for them. In Jesus' day, Rome appointed the high priest; but the Sadducee Annas had so much influence and wealth that he made sure that six of his sons succeeded him, and his son-in-law, Caiaphas, too. There were thousands of Sadducees but, as they were concentrated in Jerusalem, Jesus had little to do with them until the end of His life. It was Caiaphas and the Sanhedrin who were responsible for His death.

The Sanhedrin was the supreme Jewish court or council. It held court in the Temple area of Jerusalem and even had its own police. The high priest was its president, and besides him it had seventy members. The chief priests and Sadducees got the best positions on the Sanhedrin, naturally, but it also included both 'elders' – rich and influential men, who were usually Pharisees – and 'scribes'.

Most of the time, Jesus was surrounded by ordinary people, but on one occasion one of the Jerusalem 'aristocracy' came to visit Him: Nicodemus. We know three things about this man. He was wealthy. After Jesus' crucifixion, he brought a mixture of myrrh and aloes to be buried with His body – several stone in weight and worth a lot of money! He was a Pharisee, who would have lived his life observing every detail of the religious law. And he was a member of the elite Sanhedrin.

John 3 tells us that Nicodemus came to see Jesus at night. It's amazing he came at all, given who he was. Why at night? Maybe he was busy in the daytime. Rabbis believed that the night was the best time to study so you wouldn't be disturbed. Maybe he wanted some privacy with Jesus, with no crowds milling around. Most likely, as a man of his position, he was afraid to be seen associating with Jesus. When he told Him he was impressed by the signs and wonders He had been doing, Jesus explained that these were not important. What mattered was 'being born anew' or (the Greek word can mean this as well) 'being born from above'. To be born anew is to be so changed inside that it is like a rebirth or a recreation.

Nicodemus didn't understand the expression 'born anew'. He was an old man, after all! Jesus was sad that an expert in the Scriptures had misunderstood what the prophets had said about the coming Messiah. So, did Nicodemus leave Jesus the same man as he had come? Certainly, he still seemed to be afraid to let his deeper feelings be known to his fellow Pharisees.

In John 7:50 we find Nicodemus finally fronting up to the other Pharisees. Jesus is preaching at the Feast of Tabernacles and the crowds are saying that He is either a prophet or the Messiah. The chief priests and the Pharisees tell the Temple police to arrest Him, but they return empty-handed, saying they've never heard anyone speaking the way Jesus does. The Pharisees are not impressed. 'Have any of the leading Jews or any of *us* believed in this charlatan?' they sneer. Nicodemus must have just stood in silence. 'No,' they continue. 'Only the ignorant masses believe in him, damn them!'

It is at this point we hear a timid protest from Nicodemus. He raises the question of justice and legality. 'Does our law condemn anyone without first hearing them? Do we judge a man without giving him a chance to defend himself?' The other Pharisees sneer at him, too. 'Are you a Galilean like him? Look it up – no prophet ever came from Galilee!' (Hang on, Pharisees, try to get your facts right! I believe Jonah did!) Nicodemus again goes into mute mode. I think his heart is telling him to stick up for Jesus but his head is telling him not to take the risk. No one says it's easy to be a believer when surrounded by non-believers.

The next time Nicodemus may have been involved with Jesus is when He is sentenced to death by the high priest, Caiaphas, and the Sanhedrin is asked to ratify his decision. Was Nicodemus absent when the council voted to have Jesus crucified, or did he just stay silent like before?

Calvary changed him, however. When Jesus was dead, Nicodemus and another secret disciple, a prominent member of the Sanhedrin called Joseph of Arimathea, went public and asked Pilate if they could have the body for burial. They no longer cared what anybody thought. Joseph gave Jesus his own tomb while Nicodemus gave Him burial clothes and spices enough for a king.

In the end, Nicodemus discovered a higher and greater authority than the Law. From then on, he wanted to be known as a follower of Jesus. He now understood what He had said that night. Being born anew meant having a brand new start in life, just like a newborn baby. No longer could Nicodemus be a silent believer. This new life demanded that he showed his true colours. Christian tradition says that he died a martyr some time in the first century.

Charity begins at home. Not.

KEY VERSE

'[Jesus] came to Nazareth where he had been reared. As he always did on the Sabbath, he went to the meeting place.' Luke 4:16 (The Message)

JESUS WAS BECOMING quite a celebrity around Galilee. He was doing a tour of the local synagogues and both He and His message were being well received. In fact, the Bible tells us His listeners were actually praising Him. With things going so well, He decided to go back to His home town, Nazareth. Maybe He was expecting a similar reception there from those who had known Him and His family for many years. There He would run into old friends and acquaintances with whom He had grown up and even worked for while involved with His father's carpentry business.

Maybe you think of Nazareth as a small town, but there may have been as many as 20,000 people living there in Jesus' day. As a child, He must have been taught the history of the area – and it had a lot of history! I can imagine Him sitting on top of one of the surrounding hills, gazing into the distance and thinking about all the amazing things that had happened there in years gone by.

It was in that area that Deborah and Barak had fought in the twelfth century BC. Not long afterwards, Gideon had won his victories there. Nearby, King Saul had committed suicide, the good King Josiah was killed and the wicked Queen Jezebel had met her end. Also in view were Mount Carmel, where Elijah had had his dramatic contest with the prophets of Baal, and Shunem, where Elisha had lived. And, far away in the distance, on a clear day the blue of the Mediterranean Sea could be seen! It was a very interesting area for the young Jesus to grow up in.

But now Jesus is returning to His home town not as a young boy but as a thirty-year-old rabbi. It is a journey He is making alone, as He has not yet chosen His disciples. On the Saturday, the Jewish Sabbath, Jesus goes into the synagogue, in accordance with His usual practice. The service is divided into three sections. First comes the worship, when the congregation sing or chant (unaccompanied by any musical instruments) and pray to God. Then, some scriptures are read, and then comes the teaching, followed by discussion. On this occasion, a scroll of Scripture is handed to Jesus, so He stands up and begins to read from Isaiah 61, as follows (in my paraphrase):

> 'I am filled with the Holy Spirit.
> I am here to preach good news to the poor.
> I am here to show prisoners how they can be set free.
> I am here to give sight to those who can't see.
> I am here to help those who are suffering.'

He then rolls up the scroll and sits down to teach. (In those days, that's how they did things.) He tells the congregation that today this old prophecy has come true. It was written about Him! Up until this point, everyone has seemed happy with what Jesus has been saying. They think His words have been very gracious. But this pulls them up short.

'Hang on!' they think. 'This is just Joseph the carpenter's son! What gives Him the right to say such things?'

Jesus realises that He is not going to go down as well in Nazareth as He has elsewhere in Galilee, so He remarks that no prophet is accepted in his home town. Still, He goes on with His sermon – and the longer He goes on, the angrier His listeners become. He is saying things they do not want to hear. The Jews had no time for Gentiles, but Jesus observes that there are non-Jews who have more faith than anyone who is listening to Him now. He explains that, unlike other places He has visited, He can't do any miracles here in His home town because people here don't believe in Him. He then proves His point that God has time for non-Jews with a couple of illustrations from their Old Testament heroes. There were many Jewish widows in Israel, He says, but Elijah chose to stay with a Gentile widow from Sidon. And in Elisha's day there were many Jews suffering from leprosy, but Elisha chose to heal another Gentile, Naaman the Syrian.

The congregation have heard enough and they explode with anger. They manhandle Jesus out of the synagogue and drag Him out of the town until they come to a steep drop. They aim to push Him over the cliff and kill Him. But somehow they are not able to do this and Jesus walks right through them to safety. He has only just begun the work God has planned for Him, and what a start! Not just verbally abused by so-called old friends of the family but also physically abused by a mob intent on murdering Him! From this point onwards, Jesus knows that what God has called Him to do is not going to be easy. Of course, there are some very happy times ahead, times of great rejoicing and celebration along the way; but being obedient to God is going to present major challenges as well.

I am so grateful to God that one of the first messages from Jesus recorded in Scripture is one where He says He hasn't come just to bring His gospel to the Jews, it is intended for everyone – which includes you and me.

All of us, young and old, are called by God – not just to share the good news of Jesus but to *be* that good news to the people we meet. Some of the hardest places to do this are with our family, our workmates and our non-believing close friends. They know us too well. They can remember some of the wrong things we have done in the past, and sometimes they remind us of them. They quote that dreadful saying 'Can a leopard change its spots?', implying that a person can never change. Well, in fact a leopard *can* change its spots – but it takes a miracle to do so. A person *can* see their lives changed from bad to good. It takes a miracle to do it – but on the cross Jesus performed the miracle that makes it possible.

Another hard place to share and be the good news is in our home town. We often hear wonderful stories of God doing amazing things from Christians who travel overseas to minister in other countries. I think that's why so many people love doing ministry abroad. Sadly, a lot fewer Christians seem to have a heart for the community in which they actually live. Why? Because it's harder to serve there, and yes, like Jesus we may not be accepted. We tend to leave local evangelism to our vicars, pastors, youth leaders and so on – those who are on the church payroll and are employed to work locally. And yet, even though there isn't much glitz and glamour in this kind of evangelism, I personally find great satisfaction in doing it.

Remember that in Acts 1:8 the last words Jesus spoke before His ascension were: 'You will be my witnesses in Jerusalem [where you live], and in all Judea and Samaria [further away], and to the ends of the earth.' Maybe we should all get our basic training by evangelising in our own Nazareth, our home town, before we set out to try and evangelise the rest of the world.

Loving father, lousy parent!

KEY VERSE

'*For the Lord corrects* and *disciplines everyone whom He loves, and He punishes, even scourges, every son whom He accepts* and *welcomes to His heart and cherishes.*' Hebrews 12:6 (Amplified Bible)

DAVID IS WELL known for so many good things he achieved in life, but whenever his name is mentioned, most people remember one bad thing he did. He was tempted when he saw a naked woman bathing, and had sex with her. Bathsheba was her name and David sleeps with her knowing perfectly well that she is married to Uriah, a Hittite officer who has served him loyally for years and in 2 Samuel 23 is even listed as one of his thirty-seven 'mighty men'. Bathsheba falls pregnant and so – to avoid a scandal – David summons Uriah back from the front and tries to get him to sleep with her without delay, so that everyone will take it for granted the child is his. When Uriah declines to go home to sleep with his wife in his own bed while the rest of the army is still out in the field, fighting a war, David makes sure that he is killed in battle.

God is very unhappy about this. David realises that he has done wrong and confesses his sin and God forgives him. Nonetheless, He says that David will be punished: the child conceived in immorality will die. Soon after he is born, his new son becomes ill. David pleads with God to let him live and, in an attempt to make Him change His mind, he stops eating and spends the nights lying on the ground on sackcloth. Seven days later, the baby dies. When David is told, he gets up, washes, dresses, worships God and breaks his fast. As long as the baby was still alive, he tells his servants, there was a hope that the Lord would change His mind; but now it's over. David loved that tiny baby but sadly sometimes the innocent suffer for the guilty. David comforts Bathsheba (who by now is his wife) and in due course she bears him another son, who is called Solomon.

But then we have the sordid stories of David's other sons. They're not easy reading for the faint-hearted! David's eldest son, Amnon, falls madly in love with his very pretty half-sister Tamar. He is so full of frustrated lust for her it makes him ill. Tamar is a virgin and it seems impossible for Amnon to get what he wants. David's nephew Jonadab – 'a very shrewd man', we are told – is a mate of Amnon and asks him why he is so miserable. When Amnon tells him, Jonadab suggests that he should go to bed pretending to be ill and ask if Tamar could bring him something to eat. David goes to see him in his room and gives permission for Tamar to visit him. When she arrives with some food, Amnon grabs hold of her. She begs him not to do anything – if he asks the king, she says, they could get permission to get married – but Amnon just goes ahead and rapes her. Once he's done, he finds that he hates Tamar more than he ever loved her. She pleads with him not to send her away, but he gets a servant to throw her out, distraught and destroyed. Tamar's brother Absalom finds her weeping. He comforts her and tells her not to take this thing to heart, but of course there is no way he is going to let it go himself. David is furious but it seems he does nothing to discipline Amnon. Sons meant much more than daughters in those days, after all.

Absalom bides his time for two years, until one day he decides to have a party with his sheep-shearing friends. These were always wild, boozy occasions and he invites his father and his brothers to come. David declines the invitation, saying that it would be too much for Absalom if they all went, but encourages his sons to go. It's payback time for Amnon. Once the party is in full swing and Absalom sees that Amnon is very drunk, he shouts to the shearers, 'Kill him!' and they do just that. The other brothers run for their lives. Absalom goes into hiding, while David weeps bitterly over the death of Amnon. One wonders whether Absalom would ever have done such a thing if David had punished Amnon properly for the rape.

Absalom is exiled, but after three years David longs to see him again. He allows him to come back to Jerusalem but refuses to see him for a further two years. Meanwhile, Absalom has had a daughter himself and named her Tamar after his ruined sister. Eventually, father and son appear to be reconciled. However, within a short while Absalom rebels and raises an army, hoping to take his father's throne. David is told that his people favour Absalom, so he flees the city rather than confront his son. He leaves ten of his concubines to take care of the palace. Absalom arrives in Jerusalem and decides to sleep with his father's concubines, to show everyone how little he respects him.

David has assembled a large army to deal with Absalom, but he tells his officers to be gentle with the young man for his sake. David's army wins the ensuing battle. Absalom takes off on a mule but as he is riding past an oak tree his long hair gets tangled in some low branches and he is left hanging helplessly as his mule ploughs on. David's commanding officer, Joab, plunges three spears into his heart and then his soldiers finish him off. David is heartbroken at the news of Absalom's death. 'If only I had died instead of him!' he keeps saying. His rebellious son had meant more to him than all his wives, his concubines, his army and even himself.

David is now very old – and cold! There were no hot water bottles in those days, so he is warmed in bed by a beautiful young woman called Abishag. No sexual activity takes place, however. Adonijah, yet another of his sons, decides that it is time he was king. He is the eldest son now that Absalom is dead, and a fine figure of a man as well! He starts raising an army, but his father no longer seems to care. However, Bathsheba hears what Adonijah is up to and she goes in to see David and reminds him that he had promised that her son, Solomon, would succeed him.

David agrees and has Solomon anointed and proclaimed king in his place. When Adonijah hears of this, he is afraid for his life and begs Solomon to pardon him – which he does.

When David dies, Adonijah persuades Bathsheba that he is in love with Abishag (his father's hot water bottle) and asks her if she could ask Solomon if he could marry her, as a kind of consolation prize for losing the kingdom. Solomon immediately sees that this is a cunning plan to get the throne back, so he has Adonijah killed.

There is no getting around it. While so many victories were being won on the battlefield, one disaster after another was happening in David's home. One of the great things about the Bible is that it doesn't just tell us about people's strong points and good deeds and how well they served God. It's very honest and we also read about their weaknesses and failings. Not least, we learn that David was a loving father but not so hot with his parenting skills! Have you ever felt a bit like him? I know I have. We let things go when we should act, and sometimes we act when we should let things go!

David was far from perfect but, as we read in Acts 13:22, he was a man after God's own heart. Those of us who are parents are not going to get everything right in dealing with our children. We need to ask God for

His wisdom to help us in this, and in remembering that to love means to discipline. I think it's even more important that we try to be people after God's own heart. If we can achieve that *and* learn from David's mistakes, hopefully it will make us better parents as well.

Even the bad times are good

KEY VERSE

'I'm hurt and in pain; Give me space for healing, and mountain air.' Psalm 69:29 (The Message)

I KNOW I'M having a really bad day if I feel the need to read the book of Job to cheer myself up! I'm still searching for a Bible verse that says 'Love the Lord your God and you'll never have a bad day'. The opposite so often seems to be the case.

Let's have a brief look at Moses and Paul, two of God's superheroes who, although very different in most respects, both knew what it was to have a hard time. Moses spent a lot of his life watching other people suffer. He watched an Egyptian suffer as he killed him. He watched the Israelites suffer as slaves in Egypt. He watched the Egyptians suffer from bloody water, frogs, gnats or lice, flies, cattle disease, boils, hail, locusts, unnatural darkness and the death of their firstborn sons. He watched Pharaoh's pursuing forces suffer as they drowned in the Red Sea. He watched the Amalekite and Israelite armies suffer as he raised or lowered his staff on top of a hill. He watched as the Levites killed three thousand people for worshipping a golden calf. He watched as the mutinous Korah, Dathan and Abiram and their families were swallowed up by the earth and as fire killed another 250 prominent Israelite men who had followed Korah's lead. He watched as a further 14,700 grumblers were struck down by plague. And finally he watched as many impatient Israelites died from snakebites before he stuck a bronze snake on a pole.

Paul had the opposite problem, if you like. While Moses watched other people suffer, other people watched Paul suffer. He was blinded when he encountered Christ. When he started preaching in Damascus, the Jews tried to kill him but he escaped in a basket lowered over the wall. In Jerusalem, some Jews tried to kill him. He was banned from Antioch. He was almost stoned in Iconium. In Lystra, he *was* stoned and was left for dead outside the city. In Philippi, he was put in prison and then locked in the stocks. In

Ephesus, he 'fought with wild beasts' (whether literally or figuratively). Back in Jerusalem, he was almost beaten to death, and was then punched in the mouth in the Sanhedrin. On one occasion, more than forty Jews conspired to kill him. In Caesarea, he spent more than two years in jail. He was bitten by a snake in Malta. Finally, after several years' imprisonment in Rome, he was (probably) beheaded on Nero's orders.

And that's not all. As he puts it himself in 2 Corinthians 11:23–27 (according to *The Message*):

'I've worked much harder [than any "pseudo-apostle"], been jailed more often, beaten up more times than I can count, and at death's door time after time. I've been flogged five times with the Jews' thirty-nine lashes, beaten by Roman rods three times, pummeled with rocks once. I've been shipwrecked three times, and immersed in the open sea for a night and a day.

'In hard traveling year in and year out, I've had to ford rivers, fend off robbers, struggle with friends, struggle with foes. I've been at risk in the city, at risk in the country, endangered by desert sun and sea storm, and betrayed by those I thought were my brothers.

'I've known drudgery and hard labor, many a long and lonely night without sleep, many a missed meal, blasted by the cold, naked to the weather.'

'Die Hard' would be the perfect title for Paul's life's story, but he makes Bruce Willis look very tame. Sure, he did like to boast a bit, but if anyone had a right to boast, I guess he did!

So, did Moses have it easier than Paul? Probably not. It's sometimes more painful watching other people suffer, rebel against God or die than suffering yourself.

When we consider the God of the Old Testament and the God of the New, it is hard sometimes to believe that they are the same God. In the Old Testament, we often find God's people watching as He fights their battles for them supernaturally. In the New Testament, we often find God watching as His people fight their own battles. In the Old Testament, God seems to love those who obey Him and punish those who don't. In the New Testament, He loves those who obey Him and also those who don't, whom He tells us we must love, too. God now wants us to love our enemies instead of hurting or killing them. Maybe some of us wish we were still in Old Testament times, as getting revenge seems much more satisfying than showing forgiveness.

But why the big change? Obviously, Jesus' life, death and resurrection replaced law with grace. Instead of taking an eye for an eye, God now wants us to walk hand in hand. But Pentecost, too, played a major part in equipping His servants to make this change. In the Old Testament, God's Spirit came upon people only temporarily, when they needed to do something superhuman.

A good example is Samson. The Spirit of the Lord enabled him to tear a lion to pieces, to kill 30 men from Ashkelon, to kill a thousand Philistine men with an ass's jawbone and, finally, to bring down the temple of Dagon on the heads of several thousand Philistine men and women. After Pentecost, the Spirit no longer gave God's people the power to destroy, but the power to do miracles, to heal the sick and, contrary to human nature, to love those who persecuted them. After Pentecost, the Spirit no longer came upon God's people temporarily, but made His home within them.

Today, we realise how feeble we are. We know we cannot face hard times without asking for God's help, and certainly we cannot love our enemies or make it through our worst days without calling for the aid of the Holy Spirit within us. But the great news is that that is exactly what He wants us to do. It is only by constantly asking the Holy Spirit within for assistance that we can ever face our daily challenges and be 'more than conquerors'.

Let's finish with the encouraging words of Paul from Romans 5:3–5 (according to *The Message*):

'We continue to shout our praise even when we're hemmed in with troubles, because we know how troubles can develop passionate patience in us, and how that patience in turn forges the tempered steel of virtue, keeping us alert for whatever God will do next.

'In alert expectancy such as this, we're never left feeling shortchanged. Quite the contrary – we can't round up enough containers to hold everything God generously pours into our lives through the Holy Spirit!'

A peek at a deacon!

KEY VERSE

'[A deacon] must keep hold of the deep truths of the faith with a clear conscience.' 1 Timothy 3:9

FOR MOST OF my life I have been in some form of leadership in non-traditional churches, but when I was a young lad I was a choirboy in our local parish church. When I started worshipping in Chichester Cathedral, it was very different from anything else I had experienced over the years, of course – but, strange as it may sound, I found it very refreshing and it led me into some new areas in my walk with God. But I encountered a slight problem.

For most of my Christian life, I have had a travelling ministry and up until then I had always been part of a team, receiving input from people in leadership. I had no idea how this might be possible in a cathedral, so I went and saw the Bishop to find out if he had any suggestions. He said something I never expected to hear. He asked me whether I had ever considered being ordained and becoming part of the cathedral team as a permanent deacon. (Which meant that I would remain a deacon and not go on to become a priest.) As a travelling evangelist who had been in leadership in nearly all the churches I had attended, I didn't feel that it was God's plan for me to become a parish priest. A permanent deacon sounded perfect!

I had to undergo a lot of very intensive training, but in time I was ordained as the missioner/evangelist deacon at the cathedral. It's a role I love, because as a deacon my principal calling is to take the church to the world and bring the world to the church – which is what I have been trying to do all my Christian life. At Communion services, I wear my stole across one shoulder, to remind me what Jesus taught about staying humble, treating everyone as better than myself and being willing to wash people's feet, however dirty they might be!

It was around AD 34, just a couple of years after Jesus had ascended into heaven and the Holy Spirit had come down and filled the believers at Pentecost. The Early Church had only recently been formed and very quickly, like most churches, it had run into difficulties. I have discovered that when God is pouring out His blessing on a church, you can expect to encounter problems. Let's face it, there are always likely to be problems when you get a group of people together from different backgrounds and with different personalities! Some of the three thousand foreign Jews who became followers of Jesus after Peter's inspired preach at Pentecost remained in Jerusalem and joined the church the apostles were overseeing there.

Now, in those very early days, the Church had two kinds of members. First, there were the Hebraic Jews, who were very traditional and spoke Hebrew and Aramaic. And then there were the Grecian Jews, also known as 'Hellenists', who spoke Greek and had forgotten their Hebrew and really were more Greek than Hebrew. As in any congregation, there were a number of widows who had to be provided for. Each one received a daily distribution of food, but the poor Grecian Jews were getting less than the other widows.

At this time, Jesus' apostles were responsible for everything that happened in church life and it was only now, it seems, that it dawned on them that they had taken on far too much and it was time to delegate some tasks to others. Leadership is about teamwork. A one-man ministry, or maybe even a twelve-man ministry in this case, was not going to work. The Church is about allowing people with different God-given talents and ministries to exercise them.

The apostles decided that their priority was to commit themselves to prayer and preaching and teaching the Word of God, and so they called together a group of men and women whom they trusted and told them to choose seven men from among their number to oversee the practical matters and deal with the practical problems as they arose. What qualities should they look for? Well, these men had to be full of the Holy Spirit and wisdom. The apostles were not looking for theologians, academics or great preachers for this important administrative role.

Seven men were duly chosen, and – surprise, surprise! – they all had Greek names. Which was ideal when it came to making sure that from now on the Grecian Jewish widows got their fair share of food. These men were given the title 'deacon', which meant simply that their job was to care for people and serve them. The apostles laid hands on them and commissioned them for their ministry, which was like my own ordination. I knelt before God and as the Bishop addressed me as 'Deacon Ish' (which is how I am now known) and placed his hands on my head, I felt an amazing power of the Holy Spirit flow through me.

One of the seven was a man called Philip. After Stephen had been martyred, persecution overcame the Early Church and it was scattered. We read that Deacon Philip went to Samaria and did many wonderful miracles, including healing the sick and casting out unclean spirits. Many people were saved, including a certain Simon the Sorcerer. The apostles Peter and John were called in as bishops or elders to confirm the revival that Philip was heading up. So, now we have Deacon Philip who is also a preacher and revivalist!

As the revival continued, an angel took Philip out of it and told him to go south. In Gaza, he intercepted a chariot carrying the Queen of Ethiopia's chief treasurer, who was reading what Isaiah says about 'the suffering servant' but couldn't understand it. Philip explained to him the meaning of the scripture, prayed for his salvation and then baptised him. So, now it's Deacon Philip the Bible teacher and personal evangelist! The Spirit then flew him to Azotus, and from there he travelled from town to town all the way up to Caesarea. So, now he's a travelling evangelist. Finally, in Acts 21 we read that Philip settled down in Caesarea and became a local evangelist. He probably stayed put for 25 years. In that time he had four daughters, who all grew up to become prophetesses – so he must have been a pretty good father to have brought his daughters up so well.

It was in Caesarea that Paul and Luke stayed with him in AD 58 on Paul's last, fateful journey to Jerusalem. Philip and Paul had a lot in common – especially a concern to share the good news with Gentiles.

It is thought that Deacon Philip ended up being the Bishop of Lydia. So, Deacon Philip was a pastor/deacon, then a revivalist preacher, then a teacher and evangelist, then a bishop/elder/overseer. So, be warned! God can lead us into varied and even unexpected ministries. Like Philip, we just need to be open to be used by God in every situation in which we find ourselves. It makes the Christian life even more exciting!

❱ That's the Spirit!

KEY VERSE 'Be filled and *stimulated with the [Holy] Spirit.'* Ephesians 5:18 (Amplified Bible)

WHEN I READ some parts of the Bible, I try and imagine that I'm not only there but I'm one of the characters in the story. Having a very vivid imagination really helps. For the start of this study, I'm going to pretend that I am the apostle Peter. Here goes …

I have to admit, I've had some great times as I've walked around following Jesus. I've seen Him heal at least twenty-seven people, some blind, some deaf, some even lepers. I've seen Him do at least nine impossible things, including making 180 gallons of the best wine out of water and feeding over five thousand people with five buns and two sardines. I've seen Him make at least six mad people sane – one of them so mad he used to live in a graveyard. I've seen Him bring at least three people back to life when they were definitely dead. One of those had already been buried for four days! And those are just a few of the many amazing things I've seen.

Everything seemed to be going so well for three years – and then suddenly, disaster. Let me tell you what happened over the saddest week ever. Things started to go wrong from the Saturday. That day, we arrived in Bethany for supper with Jesus' friends Lazarus, Mary and Martha. As usual, Judas spoiled the party by moaning about Mary pouring some expensive perfume over Jesus. On Sunday, a massive crowd went wild shouting 'Hosanna!' ('Save us!') as Jesus rode into Jerusalem on a donkey. I could see that some of the religious bigwigs were not at all happy about that. On Monday, Jesus caused a rumpus in the Temple by throwing some money-traders out. He said they had no right to be doing business in there. Tuesday He spent in teaching and telling us wonderful stories. Wednesday was a quiet day spent with our friends back in Bethany.

On Thursday, everything started to go really wrong. We had a very solemn supper and Jesus said that Judas had betrayed Him. A short while later, as we were resting in Gethsemane while Jesus prayed, we were surprised by the Temple police and they arrested Him! That night, I did something I never, ever thought I would do – I denied that I was a friend of Jesus. Three times. I felt terrible about it. Jesus was tried and condemned to death and on the Friday He was nailed up on a cross. Of course, I never thought He actually *would* die, as He's the Messiah – but to my horror He did.

I can't even bring myself to tell you how I felt the next day. Everything I believed in and had lived for for the past three years was finished. The greatest man I had ever met was dead. The word 'depressed' doesn't even begin to cover how I was feeling. But then Sunday came. Some of our women discovered that the tomb in which Jesus had been buried was empty! John and I ran down there to take a look. Jesus had come back from the dead – and if you check out Luke 24:34 you'll see He came and saw me personally.

The next forty days were brilliant, just like old times! Jesus hung out with us and even cooked us breakfast on the beach. He showed Himself to hundreds of other people as well, so that no one could doubt He really was alive. During this time, He told us we weren't ready yet to do what He'd got planned for us. You see, as long as we were with Him we were fine, but when we were on our own again we were still very scared. We lacked power and boldness and Jesus told us we must wait in Jerusalem until we received them. I hadn't a clue what He meant, of course, but if Jesus said it I knew something special was about to happen.

Soon after that, we saw Jesus rise up into the sky, right into the clouds! As we stood there, staring in amazement, two men dressed in white asked us what we thought we were doing. They told us we had seen Jesus go up into heaven and one day He would return in the same way. We went back to John Mark's mum's house, just outside Jerusalem, and waited there, because the Pentecost celebrations – fifty days after Passover – were only ten days away. We were all still quite frightened, because it was very possible that any of Jesus' followers who were caught would be put to death.

While we were waiting, about 120 of us held our first church meeting. We decided we needed a replacement for Judas. Two men seemed to fit the bill, Joseph and Matthias, so we prayed about it and then someone wrote their names on two stones and we put them in a jar and shook it up and down. Matthias's stone was the first to come out, so he became the twelfth apostle. Looking back, I wonder whether maybe we should have waited until Paul arrived on the scene, six years later.

Anyway, the Day of Pentecost arrived and me and the other lads, being good Jews, went to nine o'clock prayers in Solomon's Porch in the Temple. Suddenly, from out of nowhere, it seemed, we heard a roaring noise like a violent wind and it looked as if tongues of fire descended on us. At that very moment, we were filled with the Holy Spirit and started speaking in languages we didn't even know. Suddenly, all our fear disappeared and we burst out into the street, praising God in all these different languages! Some people accused us of being drunk, but that was just crazy. Whoever's heard of someone who has drunk too much becoming *more* intelligible? We weren't slurring our words, we were speaking fluently in languages we'd never learned!

Anyway, filled with the Holy Spirit, I preached about Jesus and 3,000 people or so accepted the message of salvation and were baptised. Some of them took the good news back to Rome and planted a church there. From that day on, the world would never be the same. The power Jesus had had been given to us, His followers!

And now back to today. We who follow Jesus still need to be filled, and keep being refilled, with the same Holy Spirit, for three main reasons. The first and most important is to help us to praise Jesus and learn more about Him. The second is to give us the power to be effective witnesses for Him. And the third is to enable us to pass on those supernatural gifts to others, so that people don't just hear about the power of Jesus but actually see it in action!

The big, strong, weak giant

KEY VERSE

*'The Lord will give [unyielding and impenetrable]
strength to His people; the Lord will bless His people
with peace.' Psalm 29:11 (Amplified Bible)*

THE FIRST JOB I had after I left school at the age of fifteen was as a farm labourer. Being a puny ex-schoolkid, I soon discovered what little strength I had compared to the hardened older farmhands I was working alongside. I also found that lifting bales of hay and straw onto a trailer with a pitchfork demanded as much skill as muscle-power. But when lorries arrived loaded with plastic sacks full of artificial fertiliser which had to be carried into a barn – hey, that really *was* a challenge.

But as the months went by, so my strength grew and within a couple of years I was able to match my strongest workmates. I even did quite well in the competitions we had to see who could carry a sack of sugar beet the furthest – and it really was very large and very heavy!

'Sussex-born, Sussex-bred,

Strong in the arm, weak in the head.'

(OK, to be accurate I was Bristol-born – but very much Sussex-bred.) Yep, I grew strong in the arm but I was very insecure. I lodged with the farmer and his wife and family. They were all lovely people, but I felt so unsure of myself in other people's company that in the evenings I refused to join them in the lounge and preferred to spend my time alone in my bedroom. Even being with them at breakfast was hard for me. Maybe that's why even today I find it difficult sometimes to accept an invite for an evening meal in someone's house. But ever since those days on the farm I've remained fairly strong and until recently, when he started lifting weights in the local gym, I was usually a match even for my eldest son.

There are very few people in the Bible who were as physically strong as Goliath of Gath. Samson was strong but he was no giant, and he was strong only when the Spirit of God was on him. Goliath was strong all the time. At ten-and-a-half feet tall, he was the sort of guy you wouldn't want to upset – or meet on a dark night! His armour weighed fourteen stone, and just the blade of his spear weighed twenty-five pounds. No wonder King Saul and the other Israelites were terrified of him.

Let's take a quick look at his background. Deuteronomy 2 talks about the Rephaites, a tall, strong people who were displaced from their land by the Ammonites (and the Lord). 2 Samuel 21 mentions a Goliath and other huge men who were descendants of Rapha of Gath. These giants also seem to have been slightly different from other men in that some of them, at least, had twelve fingers and twelve toes. So, Goliath, although one of the strongest men in the world, had no homeland and no roots and belonged to a people who were born freaks of nature and would soon become extinct.

What sort of occupation could Goliath choose? He had to be a soldier, really. But he could never be a normal soldier – he could never be a normal anything. The Philistines used him as a massive fighting machine, standing in front of their line of battle and every now and again letting out a roar to petrify the enemy. He wasn't exactly officer material. In 1 Samuel 17, we see that the Bible was not much impressed by him – it takes only a couple of lines to describe him, while it takes nine or ten to describe his armour!

As we read the story of David and Goliath, we notice a very strange reaction from the giant from Gath. As he looked David up and down and saw that he was 'little more than a boy, glowing with health and handsome', the Bible says, 'he despised him' (1 Samuel 17:42). Why did he react so strongly to David? Why should he hate him so on sight? Surely he had no reason to feel this way – or did he? Maybe it was because David was everything he wasn't, never had been and never would be: a normal, good-looking lad, confident in himself, his nation and his God. Goliath's only qualities were his height and strength and here he was, not even faced with a great Israelite warrior to fight.

Even if he killed this lad, he'd hardly look a hero. It would be humiliating. It was impossible for Goliath to win this battle whatever the outcome. I have a suspicion that this outwardly mighty giant maybe felt rejected and weak inside – and now he was facing his own giant. He didn't lose the battle when he lost his head, he lost it when he faced David.

Most of us have learned how to act strong, and even how to look strong; but how strong are we really inside? There will always be times when we have to face someone and our hidden weaknesses and feelings of rejection will begin to show. We all have our Davids to face and we all have insecurities we need to overcome.

Our Bible verse says: 'The Lord will give strength to His people; the Lord will bless His people with peace.' I don't believe that true strength is measured by the ability to lift a quarter-ton dumb-bell or knock a ten-foot giant out and chop his head off. True strength consists in being able to overcome our weaknesses and insecurities, and this can only be done with God's help. Let's allow His power which is at work within us to make us truly strong. We will still have to face our Davids, but with God's help we need never lack confidence as we do so!

# An angle on angels

KEY VERSE *'Isn't it obvious that all angels are sent to help out with those lined up to receive salvation?' Hebrews 1:14 (The Message)*

I'VE ALWAYS WANTED to meet an angel. A few years ago, when I was feeling pretty hurt by a situation at church, I used to go on regular prayer walks around a lake. The more I did this, the more I became convinced that at a particular point an angel was not just watching over me but was physically waiting for me. Every time I walked past that point I would suddenly turn, hoping to get a glimpse of him. I've still not seen him, but I'll keep looking.

Let's spend a little time looking at angels in the Bible. The first thing we need to get clear in our minds is that Jesus was never just a superior angel. He is the Son of God and that puts Him in a different league entirely. Angels were never referred to as God's sons, and when Jesus was born in Bethlehem we know that the angels were very excited about this and worshipped Him. However, angels did play a major role in the life of Jesus while He was on earth.

It was an angel who told old Zechariah that he was to have a son called John. It was an angel who told young Mary that she was to give birth to the Lord Jesus. It was an angel who told Joseph what was happening with Mary. After Jesus was born and King Herod started killing little boys, it was an angel who warned Joseph to flee with his family to Egypt. As Jesus faced temptation at the beginning of His public ministry, it was angels who protected Him and ministered to Him after Satan had done his worst. Jesus knew He was never alone and when some villagers had been unpleasant to Him and James and John wanted to call down fire from heaven, He reminded them that there was no need for that – He had ten thousand angels with Him!

In the Garden of Gethsemane, angels were present to help Jesus through His agony of mind. But when Jesus was on the cross the angels could only watch. They could do nothing unless He cried out for their help. At the resurrection we see that angels have amazing strength, as it took only one of them to roll away a tombstone that would have weighed well over a ton. It was an angel who passed on the great news to Jesus' followers that He was alive. As Jesus disappeared into the clouds at the ascension, it was angels who asked His disciples why they were staring at the sky and told them He would be coming back.

So, we can see that angels played some major roles in the life of Jesus and the gospel story. Some people have the wrong idea about angels, though. First of all, their appearance. We know for a fact that they don't drift around in long, white robes playing harps! When people like Abraham and Lot encountered angels, they certainly didn't recognise them as such – they talked to them as if they were men. Second, angels are not people (and especially children) who have died, however comforting the idea may be. They are a completely different order of being from humans. One can never become the other. And, third, angels are not mediators between us and God. Only Jesus is. They must not be worshipped or prayed to. On two occasions in Revelation an angel tells John: Don't fall down and worship me – I'm just a servant as you are.

So, what are angels exactly? Angels belong to an order of being between human beings and God. They are superior to us (and, according to the Bible, far more beautiful). They are stronger than us. Jacob had no hope of winning when he picked a fight with an angel! From Isaiah 37:36 we learn that a single angel was more than a match for 185,000 Assyrians. They are more intelligent than us. They know what is happening on earth and some of what is happening in heaven. And they are faster than us. When Daniel prayed, God dispatched an angel from highest heaven and it had arrived before the prophet had finished his prayer. Less than a minute, I reckon.

Here are a few biblical facts about angels. Angels are not born and cannot marry or die. There is a finite number of them. Just how many are there? The book of Revelation speaks of 'ten thousand times ten thousand' (or 'a myriad of myriads') and, on another occasion, twice that number – on horseback! Which is probably the author's way of saying he couldn't count them all. They are far inferior to God. They are His creation and they do not share His power, His knowledge or His eternity. There are different ranks of angel: archangels, cherubim, seraphim, principalities, powers … Some are given names: Gabriel, Michael and Lucifer. There are good angels and bad angels. One third of the heavenly host rebelled against God along with the archangel Lucifer.

Since the resurrection, angels have continued to serve as God's messengers. We are never told that they have all returned to heaven. Quite the opposite, in fact – they spoke to people like Philip in the earliest days of the Church, and just as an angel sprang Peter from prison, so they are still around to help us today.

So, what else do angels get up to? We read in Matthew 18:10 that every little child has an angel in heaven whose eyes are fixed on the face of God. We know that the angels rejoice when someone decides to follow Jesus. They can protect us from certain dangers, terrors and fears. Remember the story of Elisha and his servant? They can get physical and strike and destroy people who go against God. Check out Herod's demise in Acts 12:23! And from Matthew 13:40–42 we learn that one of their final tasks will be to 'weed out of' God's kingdom 'everything that causes sin and all who do evil' and throw them into the furnace.

Many people wonder if there is intelligent life 'out there'? It may be hard for us to imagine, but according to the Bible the heavens are full of beings watching humankind. A Russian cosmonaut was asked what he saw in space. 'I didn't see any angels,' he joked as he sipped his vodka. Maybe not – but you can be sure the angels saw him! Angels are not fictional beings, they are not fairies; they are messengers from God and part of their commission is to oversee you and me.

I think that's good news, don't you?

❭ This story doesn't hold water – or does it?

KEY VERSE

'Dear GOD, my Master, you created earth and sky by your great power – by merely stretching out your arm! There is nothing you can't do.' Jeremiah 32:17 (The Message)

IT HAD BEEN ten generations and 1,656 years since things had gone badly wrong for Adam and Eve, and God was not happy. We are told in Genesis 6:1–2 that 'the sons of God' had married 'the daughters of humans'. Who were these 'sons of God'? Maybe they were angels. Some think they were kings who regarded themselves as divine and set up harems. Others suggest that they were the sons of godly Seth marrying the daughters of wicked Cain. Let's face it, we really have no idea – but we do know that God was very angry that these marriages were taking place.

He saw that human hearts had turned and become totally wicked and He was sorry He had put our kind on the earth. His heart was full of pain. So, He made what I am guessing must have been a very difficult decision. He concluded that the only way to put things right was to destroy everyone – except for a man called Noah and his family. It seems that Noah was the only godly man on the face of the earth.

God began to tell Noah His plans. In a way, He was going to start afresh. He instructed Noah and his three sons, Shem, Ham and Japheth, to build a huge vessel or 'ark', shaped much like a coffin. Specifically, it had to be made of cypress wood and coated in pitch, inside and out, to make it waterproof. It was to have three decks and an overhanging roof, with a row of small windows beneath it to let in light and air. And it was to have just one door.

You can imagine Noah thinking that this floating box wouldn't need to be that big if it was just for him and his sons and their four wives. But then God gave him the dimensions: 450 feet long, 75 feet wide and 45 feet high. Or, in tabloid terms, roughly one-and-a-half football pitches long and as tall as a four-storey building. God went on to explain that He was going to flood the whole earth and only the eight members of Noah's immediate family would survive. However, they wouldn't be on their own in this monster of a boat. God was going to be sending over a few other creatures as passengers. There would be two of every kind of animal, except for the birds and the 'clean' animals, of which there would be fourteen. And there should be enough food for all of them.

Unbelievable? Well, far cleverer people than me have estimated that, with a total deck area of around 95,700 square feet, the ark would have comfortably accommodated 45,000 creatures; and a zoologist has reckoned that it must have carried 35,000-plus creatures, excluding those that could have survived outside it. Noah and his sons (and presumably other paid helpers) started building this enormous boat somewhere in Mesopotamia. It was probably a long way from any sea, in which case it's easy to imagine the ridicule they had to endure from the godless people around them. Once the ark was completed, the passengers started arriving in pairs. Unbelievable? Well, as God created all these animals and birds, it wouldn't have been too hard for Him to round them all up. And once they were all safely gathered in, He closed the door.

Then it happened. The Bible relates that 'all the springs of the great deep burst forth, and the floodgates of the heavens were opened' (Gen. 7:11). As rain has not previously been mentioned in the Bible, some people think this may have been the first time anyone had ever seen water coming down from the sky. 'By faith', says Hebrews 11:7, 'Noah, when warned about things not yet seen, in holy fear built an ark to save his family.' The 'things not yet seen' could refer to rain or a flood or, of course, something else. That doesn't matter, though. The important thing is that the water continued rising until it was twenty feet higher than the highest mountain. This was God's judgment on a wicked world.

However, God's judgment is followed by His redemption. After 150 days, He decided that that was enough and He sent a strong wind over the earth and the waters began to subside. It's generally thought that the ark floated about 500 miles and ended up on Mount Ararat, a 17,000-foot mountain in what is now Turkey, close to the Russian border. In total, Noah and his family and their thousands of passengers had spent a year and a week in the ark: five months afloat and seven on the mountainside waiting for the water to go down. When the ground was finally dry, God told Noah that everyone should disembark. After Noah had made a sacrifice, He set His rainbow in the sky as a sign of His covenant with the earth and every living thing that never again would He flood the planet.

It's a great story, but … is it really believable? As we have already seen, the writer of Hebrews believed it: 'By faith Noah, when warned about things not yet seen, in holy fear built an ark to save his family. By his faith he condemned the world and became heir of the righteousness that is in keeping with faith' (11:7). And the apostle Peter believed it: 'Long ago … God waited patiently in the days of Noah while the ark was being built. In it only a few people, eight in all, were saved through water' (1 Pet. 3:20); and 'he did not spare the ancient world when he brought the flood on its ungodly people, but protected Noah, a preacher of righteousness, and seven others' (2 Pet. 2:5). Most important of all, Jesus believed it: 'As it was in the days of Noah, so it will be at the coming of the Son of Man. For in the days before the flood, people were eating and drinking, marrying and giving in marriage, up to the day Noah entered the ark; and they knew nothing about what would happen until the flood came and took them all away. That is how it will be at the coming of the Son of Man' (Matt. 24:37–39).

Whether we believe it is one thing, though, and what it tells us about God is quite another!

So, does this story hold water? You make your own mind up – you don't need my help!

Questioning the Unquestionable

KEY VERSE

'Doom to you who fight your Maker – you're a pot at odds with the potter!
Does clay talk back to the potter:
"What are you doing? What clumsy fingers!"
Would a sperm say to a father,
"Who gave you permission to use me to make a baby?"
Or a foetus to a mother,
"Why have you cooped me up in this belly?"
Thus GOD, The Holy of Israel, Israel's Maker, says:
"Do you question who or what I'm making?
Are you telling me what I can or cannot
do?"' Isaiah 45:9–11 (The Message)

SO, IS GOD saying here that we His creatures have no right to question Him? Let's set the scene.

Israel is at an all-time low. The nation has been exiled to Babylon. Isaiah then begins to prophesy to them about the King of Persia, Cyrus, who (he says) is God's 'anointed' and His 'shepherd' and many other things that until now had been said only of their own kings. Amazingly, this man is going to contribute hugely to the future of the Jews. (Which means, by the way, that he will be used indirectly to bring about the coming of the Messiah. It's interesting that Cyrus gets some 23 mentions in the Bible – far more than most of Jesus' apostles!) A pagan king an unwitting tool in the hands of the Lord? Understandably, perhaps, people question whether God would ever do such a thing. Isaiah must be wrong. This cannot be God's plan.

As our reading indicates, God was not pleased by this reaction. This raises a problem. God made us to have questioning minds and every day we question ourselves about things we have thought, said and done. And we certainly question those around us. But do we have the right to question almighty God? If we examine Scripture, we find that nearly everyone in it seems to have questioned Him at one time or another. Let's look at a few examples.

Abraham questioned God when He resolved to destroy Sodom and Gomorrah. He tried to negotiate with God, to cut a deal with Him to spare some of the people in those cities. He even questioned the morality of God's decision. Abraham questioned God but still remained His friend. Then Moses. He was mightily used in leading the children of Israel out of Egypt to the Promised Land – but initially he had a massive problem agreeing with God that he was the right man for the job. He tried to convince the God who made him that he was a poor choice, because he was not a good speaker. Moses questioned God but still remained His friend.

The Psalms are full of insistent questions addressed to God: 'How long do we have to wait until You do something?' The question 'How long?' is asked seventeen times. One man who was very direct in his questioning was Elijah. He had miraculously supplied the widow of Zarephath and her son with food when they were about to perish from hunger, and then, a short while later, the boy became sick and died! As *The Message* puts it, Elijah asked God: 'O GOD, my God, why have you brought this terrible thing on this widow who has opened her home to me? Why have you killed her son?' God listened to his prayer and restored the boy to life.

I guess that if anyone has a right to question God, it's poor old Job. And so he does, throughout his story – until God appears and starts to question him! Job questions God but still He rewards him in the end with more blessing than he'd ever had before.

Finally, two very significant people in the New Testament questioned God. The young Mary questioned God's spectacular revelation to her. How could she possibly become pregnant if she'd never had sexual relations with a man? Mary questioned God but still her cousin Elizabeth could declare that she was 'blessed among women'. And in Matthew 27 we find Jesus Himself questioning God (as *The Message* has it): 'My God, My God, why have you abandoned me?' Jesus questioned God but, as we know, the Father never stopped loving His only Son.

I guess that, like everyone in the Bible, we have all questioned God at one time or another. There have been two notable times when I questioned God. The first was when I was diagnosed with leukaemia. Strange as it may seem, I didn't ask God why He had allowed me to get leukaemia; but I did ask Him why He didn't heal me just through prayer. Like you, maybe, I have seen people healed supernaturally by prayer alone. Why did I have to go through three years of chemotherapy? Years later, I have got some sort of answer. The cancer changed my life – and that included my ministry. I now spend a lot of time with other cancer sufferers and when they are first diagnosed and feeling very scared and vulnerable I promise to 'walk their treatment journey' with them, step by step.

Many people try to help those who have cancer but find it hard to relate to their suffering, and especially the dreadful side-effects chemotherapy can have. The reason why I get on so well with cancer sufferers, and why they trust me, is that when I tell them I know exactly what they are going through and how they are feeling, they know that I honestly do. I would never have dreamed of saying that if it had not been for all those years of hospital visits and medication.

However, the time I questioned God most was when my fifteen-month-old grandson died of kidney cancer. Unlike Elijah, I couldn't charge God with killing him, but I do still question why He chose not to intervene and heal him. I must admit, I was never assured that God *would* heal him, but I was never in doubt that, being God, He could. But maybe sometimes the clay just has to trust the potter, when there seems to be no obvious answer. The way I often console myself is by repeating Isaiah 55:8–9:

'"For my thoughts are not your thoughts, neither are your ways my ways," declares the LORD. "As the heavens are higher than the earth, so are my ways higher than your ways and my thoughts than your thoughts."'

So, to sum up. It isn't a sin to question God about something, but when the people of Israel couldn't believe that God could, should or would use King Cyrus to realise His plans, they were putting themselves on the same level as God Himself. They needed to be brought down a peg or two and reminded just who God is and who they were. So, let's keep questioning – but never doubting. We should never think that we are equal with almighty God and presume to tell Him what He can or cannot do.

Another of my little poems to finish with:

'To question God is human
To doubt God is downfall,
For if our God just thinks like us
He is no God at all.'

Amazing grace

KEY VERSE

'Saving is all his idea, and all his work. All we do is trust him enough to let him do it. It's God's gift from start to finish!' Ephesians 2:8 (The Message)

TRAVELLING IN A rock band is not always as exciting as it sounds. My brother Tim and I once set off to Holland on an 'acoustic' tour. Flying was out and we had a load of gear, so it was going to be 'ferry and drive'. A supporter of my ministry had kindly given me an old Volvo estate, which for some reason he had affectionately named 'Henry'. We disembarked from the ferry and I happily drove off through fields carpeted with gorgeous, colourful flowers. In the warm sunshine, I felt compelled to sing 'Tulips from Amsterdam' – but I only knew the first line, so to my brother's annoyance I just kept singing that!

Then, surrounded by all things bright and beautiful, suddenly it all went wrong. First the oil light came on, then the engine made some strange noises and finally Henry ground to a halt and gave up the ghost. Even the tulips seemed to bow their heads in pity as we rolled into a shallow ditch by the side of the road. We were in the middle of nowhere, in a country where we couldn't speak the language and, like most Christian musicians of that era, we didn't have a guilder to our name. Everything looked hopeless. It was time to pray, even though we had no idea how God would – or even could – answer our prayers.

But He did, and pretty quickly. A friendly Dutch farmer pulled up and, after we'd explained our plight in sign language, he kindly towed us to a garage. I was thankful to God that we were no longer stuck in a lonely ditch, but weighing heavily on my mind was the thought: How on earth am I going to pay for the repairs? I can't describe my feelings of surprise and relief when I learned that a local church had heard of our situation and taken pity on us. They had had an offering for us and raised enough to cover our very expensive garage bill completely. Within a week, old Henry was cheerfully chugging along through those tulip fields with a brand-new engine and two happy musicians inside, grateful to both God and humankind!

My brother and I had done nothing to deserve that church's generosity, and that's a little like the grace of God. We haven't earned salvation, nor is it possible to earn it. It is a gift from God. Our part is simply to accept it by faith. I love the bit in Matthew 19 where, after hearing Jesus talk about rich men, camels and the eyes of needles, the disciples ask incredulously: 'Who then can be saved?' Jesus replies: 'With man this is impossible, but with God all things are possible.'

God is perfect love, and we are sinners. For Christians, sin is not so much breaking His law as breaking His heart. Let me recall, as an imperfect analogy, something that happened in London in 2000. One day, a ten-year-old boy who had only been in Britain for eleven weeks finished some study he was doing in the local library and set off home. On the way, he was (in street slang) 'jucked'. That is, he was stabbed with a broken beer bottle, which was twisted in the wound. He collapsed in a filthy stairwell and bled to death in the ambulance half an hour later.

Eventually, in August 2006, after three trials two young habitual criminals were convicted of manslaughter. They were each sentenced to eight years' youth custody, which meant that both these young men had been released by 2011, though one of them has since been recalled. By 2014, their convictions will be spent and the whole matter will be over as far as the law is concerned.

But it's not over for everyone. It isn't over for the couple whose boy they killed. The killers received a relatively short term, but they themselves sentenced that boy's parents to life without the son they loved. For someone not only to forgive their child's killer but even to show some sort of love for them may seem humanly impossible, yet Damilola's mother, Gloria Taylor, said in a BBC *Panorama* interview that she prays daily for her son's killers and asks God to touch them. This is how it is between us sinners and God. Only an act of gracious, free forgiveness on God's part can put us back into the right relationship with Him.

I have met Christians on my travels who think that accepting Christ by faith is all that is necessary for salvation. Good works don't come into it. And, according to our verse, they could be right. Good works have nothing to do with our salvation – just the grace of God and us in faith believing and receiving it.

It would be nice and uncomplicated to leave it there, but (as he often seems to do) Paul then chucks in a paradox. Having apparently discounted good works as essential to salvation, he goes on to say that there is something radically wrong with a Christian who isn't known for their good works. Let's clarify this. God loves us and we know that we don't deserve that love. We can be lovely people and spend our lives doing good things, but that will never save us or make us Christians.

However, once we receive His grace through faith and become followers of Jesus, our lives should naturally begin to change. Because we love Jesus, we should be trying our hardest to be good people and do good things for others. It is impossible to earn God's love, but we must show our gratitude for it by seeking with our whole heart to live the kind of life that will please Him. Good works cannot save us; but Paul is saying that if we *claim* to have received God's grace through faith and yet people don't see any good works, we still may not be saved!

It is not for us to judge who is or isn't a true follower of Jesus – but, still, how can we identify one? I totally believe in the supernatural gifts of the Spirit, but the Bible tells us that the hallmark of a true believer is not just that they can prophesy or speak in tongues or do miracles. This is how Eugene Peterson paraphrases Matthew 7:21–23 in *The Message*:

'Knowing the correct password – saying "Master, Master," for instance – isn't going to get you anywhere with me. What is required is serious obedience – *doing* what my Father wills. I can see it now – at the Final Judgment thousands strutting up to me and saying, "Master, we preached the Message, we bashed the demons, our God-sponsored projects had everyone talking." And do you know what I am going to say? "You missed the boat. All you did was use me to make yourselves important. You don't impress me one bit. You're out of here."'

True followers of Jesus both believe in Him and act on James 2:26: 'As the body without the spirit is dead, so faith without deeds is dead.' True followers of Jesus try to live in humility. They have nothing to brag about, after all. They know that all the credit for any good they do must go to Jesus. They try their hardest to be obedient to God and live the way He wants them to live. They often fail but, thankfully, they know the importance of genuine confession. Although far from perfect, true followers of Jesus are different from those around them. You will see in their daily living a little of the grace of God. You will see in their daily living a little of the power of God. You will see in their daily living a little of the good works of God. These are the hallmarks of the person with new life in Christ.

❭ Knees Up or Knees Down?

KEY VERSE *'So come, let us worship: bow before him, on your knees before God, who made us!' Psalm 95:6 (The Message)*

LET'S HAVE A brief look at three words: worship, praise and rejoicing. First, what are the biblical meanings of 'to worship'? The Hebrew word so translated means 'to bow down, do homage, lie prostrate'. The Aramaic word means 'to bend down, bow, stoop low'. And the Greek word means 'to come close to and kiss the hand, reverence, adore' – and also 'to honour religiously, make obeisance, serve and esteem'. For believers to offer worship to God, they must remember that they are His servants and approach Him with great humility.

In the Old Testament, we don't find too many instances of individual worship. One example we do have comes in Genesis 24:26–28, where we read that, after finding Rebekah at the well, Abraham's servant bows down and worships God saying, 'Praise be to the LORD.' However, worship seems to have taken place principally in large gatherings, as in 1 Chronicles 29:20 where David tells the whole assembly to praise God and they all bow down and prostrate themselves before Him.

Jesus makes it clear that it is not important how or where people worship, whether individually or en masse. The important thing is that we actually do genuinely worship God. And as we express the love in our hearts for our heavenly Father, those around us should see the love we have for them as well.

Today we are faced with a persistent question: What is the relationship between worship and music? And can we worship without music? Nowadays, the words 'worship' and 'music' seem almost interchangeable; but is that right or is it misleading? As we can deduce from the biblical meanings of the word, there is no direct link between worship and music in the Bible. However, a lot of Christians today – although not all, I should say – find that music can really add to their worship. Some people believe that just singing songs with spiritual lyrics is worship. It's not necessarily so. If our mouths are singing away about how much we love God but our hearts are far from Him, all we are really doing is having a good sing-song. As far as we can, we need to make sure that things are right between us and God before we start singing. If they are, then some of us may find that our voices really can add to what our hearts are already crying out.

How about praise, then? One thing I have always enjoyed doing is praising the Lord. Many years ago, I started using the term 'praise party', which many people now use to describe people of all ages giving thanks to God in a very lively and rejoicing manner! For many years, the name 'Ishmael' was synonymous with playing a guitar while dancing around the stage. Nowadays, in older years, I am still praising but, owing to lack of energy, my heart often does the dancing instead of my feet.

So, what are the biblical meanings of 'to praise'? The Hebrew words mean 'to make a noise, brag about, magnify'. (The last of these is the root meaning of the word 'hallelujah', which appears in some form in at least 200 scriptures.) They also mean 'to extend a hand, confess, give thanks' and, of course, 'make music by touching strings, striking chords, singing praises, even chanting'! The Greek words mean 'to be grateful or thankful, sing, twang or play a musical instrument'. Praise is far more than just giving thanks. It includes sacrificial offering, confession, blessing, glorifying and stretching out our hands to God. Unlike worship, however, we can see that sometimes it is directly linked to music. So, does the Bible suggest that God enjoys people praising Him with music? He certainly seems to, especially in the Old Testament, where He accepts praise that is expressed in singing, shouting and dancing and accompanied by musical instruments. In New Testament times, music doesn't seem to have been such a big deal, but we do have a few significant scriptures:

- 'Is anyone happy? Let them sing songs of praise' (James 5:13).
- 'Let the message of Christ dwell among you richly as you teach and admonish one another with all wisdom through psalms, hymns, and songs from the Spirit, singing to God with gratitude in your hearts' (Col. 3:16).
- '[Speak] to one another with psalms, hymns, and songs from the Spirit. Sing and make music from your heart to the Lord' (Eph. 5:19).
- 'Paul and Silas were praying and singing hymns to God, and the other prisoners were listening to them' (Acts 16:25).

An interesting question is: How important was music to Jesus? We will never really know the answer, of course, but we can be sure that if the Father enjoys music in worship, the Son does as well. Nonetheless, Jesus never relied on it or gave it much promotion. We know that He and His disciples sang a song in Gethsemane, but I'm guessing it wasn't a lively, upbeat one.

In Hebrews 2:11–12, we read: 'Jesus is not ashamed to call them brothers and sisters. He says, "I will declare your name to my brothers and sisters; in the assembly I will sing your praises."' (The last bit is a misquote from Psalm 22:22, which, strangely enough, doesn't actually mention any singing.)

I often think how different it would be if I were Jesus choosing twelve disciples today. A key quality I would be looking for in at least two of them would be that they were talented singers and reasonable musicians! Sadly, nowadays some Christians have become so reliant on music that they don't know how to praise God without it. Maybe it would be good to have an occasional service without any music or singing and teach people how to praise God in other ways. Although we don't read of Jesus encouraging much singing, we do know that throughout His life He encouraged worship.

Finally, what are the biblical meanings of 'to rejoice'? The Hebrew words mean 'to be glad or happy, rejoice, take pleasure, leap for joy, cry out'. The Greek words mean 'to cheer, make merry, demonstrate joy and pride by literally shouting for joy'. In short, rejoicing can be expressed by speaking, shouting, dancing, leaping, twirling, clapping and making merry in our hearts. King David presents a perfect example of uninhibited rejoicing in 2 Samuel 6!

Praising God is not only a matter of using our mouths and singing. There are many biblical ways in which both young and old worshippers can express their joy and praise to God in movement. Lifting holy hands can be an expression of thanksgiving, surrender, dependence and the offering up of our hearts. Kneeling can be an expression of humility, meekness and submission. Bowing low with our faces to the ground can be an expression of fear, respect and reverence. Lying prostrate or 'falling on our faces' can be an expression of total awe of God. Merely standing in His presence can be an expression of our acknowledgement of His majesty. Clapping our hands can be an expression of joy and thanksgiving. And dancing can just show how excited we can get about God when we're praising Him.

We can use our whole body to express our praise to God, but we must leave it to each individual how they do it. The problem so often comes when one worshipper doesn't like the way another worshipper is communicating their joy and praise, or expects everyone to express themselves in the same way they do.

Sometimes when I'm praising God, I just like to stand still or else sit down quietly. At some services when people see me doing that, either they think I'm not enjoying the music or they assume that I need some prayer and ministry! God gave us all different personalities and we must allow each individual to express themselves in a way that feels comfortable. We really shouldn't be looking at what others around us are doing.

Whatever the mouth or the body does, worship must come from the heart – and that is the part of a person only God can see.

Hey Judah, don't make it bad!

'Therefore if any person is [ingrafted] in Christ (the Messiah) he is a new creation (a new creature altogether); the old [previous moral and spiritual condition] has passed away. Behold, the fresh and new has come!' 2 Corinthians 5:17 (Amplified Bible)

MOST OF US know the story of Joseph and his Technicolor dreamcoat, either from the Bible or from the musical. The biblical story of Joseph's older brother Judah is not so well known. Jacob had twelve sons, eleven of whom gave their names to tribes of Israel: Reuben, Simeon, Levi, Judah, Issachar, Zebulun, Dan, Naphtali, Gad, Asher, Joseph and Benjamin. (The Levites were never given a territory of their own, so Joseph's two sons, Mannasseh and Ephraim, each founded a tribe to make it up to a dozen.)

All the brothers except Benjamin, who was much the youngest, were very envious of Joseph – in fact, they hated him. Their father, Jacob (or Israel), hadn't helped matters by making it very clear that Joseph was his golden boy, and Joseph himself had made things worse by telling his brothers his dreams, which always seemed to end with them bowing down to him!

Judah was the one who took charge when the eldest brother, Reuben, wasn't around, and it was Judah who suggested that, rather than kill Joseph, they should sell him to Ishmaelite slave-traders and make some money. Was he concerned to save his little brother's life or was he just pushing the 'sensible' (and profitable) option? This is, incidentally, the first reference in the Bible to someone being sold into slavery. With Joseph out of the picture and his father heartbroken by the lies he had been told, Judah moves away and marries a Canaanite woman, who gives birth to three sons: Er, Onan and Shelah.

Judah finds a wife for Er, whose name is Tamar; but Er seriously offends God, so He kills him. In accordance with the custom of the time, Judah then orders Onan to marry and sleep with his sister-in-law in order to produce an heir for his brother. (This was important because the headship or birthright of the family normally went to the firstborn son and his descendants. So, Deuteronomy 25:5–9 stipulates:

'If brothers are living together and one of them dies without a son, his widow must not marry outside the family. Her husband's brother shall take her and marry her and fulfil the duty of a brother-in-law to her. The first son she bears shall carry on the name of the dead brother so that his name will not be blotted out from Israel.

'However, if a man does not want to marry his brother's wife … [and] persists in saying, "I do not want to marry her," his brother's widow shall go up to him in the presence of the elders, … spit in his face and say, "This is what is done to the man who will not build up his brother's family line."')

Onan knows that the first son he has with Tamar won't count as his, so that his elder brother's inheritance will remain in his line, and so every time he has sex with Tamar he uses the withdrawal method of contraception to prevent her getting pregnant. But it doesn't sound as if God is angry with Onan for withdrawing early, He's angry with him for refusing to give Tamar a son while still pretending to the world that he is doing all he can. Onan's motives are simply wicked. He has sinned against his father, against Tamar but most of all against his dead brother. He is a true son of Judah because, just as his father had no love for his brother Joseph, Onan has no love for his brother Er. So, God is seriously offended by son number two and kills him, too.

Judah tells Tamar to go back to her father's house and live as a widow until Shelah is old enough to marry her. She guesses that he actually has no intention of allowing this to happen, for fear that she will be the death of Shelah, too, the only son he has left. He probably doesn't know about Onan's deceit and thinks the whole problem lies with Tamar. She knows that if she wants to have any chance of getting a son, she's going to have to take the initiative. Once Judah's wife has died and he has duly mourned her, she waits until her father-in-law is going over to Timnah to see his sheep being sheared. Then, she disguises herself with a veil and goes and sits by a roadside shrine, to all appearances a prostitute. It's a big risk, she knows.

After a long day shearing sheep, no doubt all Judah and his men want is a lads' night out, complete with booze and women. Judah sees Tamar but doesn't recognise her with her face covered. They agree that he'll pay her a young goat in return for a good time; but as he doesn't have a goat to hand, she takes his personal seal and staff as guarantees. Of course, Tamar doesn't want a goat; she just wants to get pregnant and she needs something to prove that Judah is the father. The next day, Judah sends a mate over with the goat but the prostitute has disappeared. In fact, the locals say there has never been a shrine prostitute there. By now, of course, Tamar is back in her widow's clothes at home. Judah is embarrassed that some woman has tricked him out of his seal and staff, but he decides to let it go or else he'll be a laughing-stock.

Three months later, he learns that his daughter-in-law is pregnant. As she isn't married, she stands accused of prostitution. Judah demands that she should be publicly burned alive. Why does he want her to die such a horrible death? According to Leviticus, only the very wicked should be burned alive. Prostitution wasn't punishable by death anyway, but the worst the Law of Moses might have required would be stoning. Maybe he is just desperate to get rid of her. It would save his third son ever having to marry her. Tamar shows no anger as she coolly tells him: 'See if you recognise whose seal and staff these are. The man they belong to is the father of my child.'

Judah confesses that she is more righteous than he is, given that he never made his third son marry her. The burning is now off, of course. Tamar in due course gives birth to twins. The one who is born first (though on a technicality he is actually not the firstborn) is a boy called Perez. He is to be the ancestor of David and, eventually, of Mary's husband, Joseph. It's amazing that the royal bloodline should come from the wicked Judah, not one of his righteous brothers, Joseph and Benjamin.

After all this, it seems that Judah goes back to his father's house, a changed man. There is now a famine and – unknown to his brothers – Joseph has become Pharaoh's number two. The brothers travel down to Egypt in search of food, but when they get an audience with Joseph they don't recognise him. He plays a little game with them and as a result they end up in big trouble. And now we find it's Judah pleading with Joseph for mercy. Yes, the same Judah who most hated Joseph and suggested selling him into slavery. Yes, the same Judah who unwittingly slept with his daughter-in-law and got her pregnant. Judah offers to stay in Egypt as Joseph's slave rather than break his father's heart a second time by having to tell him he'll never see Benjamin again.

So, why *did* Jesus come from Judah's line, not Joseph's? We can't be sure – but we can see that Judah was a great example of what Jesus came to achieve. He began as a hateful young man but he ended up willing to give his freedom for the sake of Benjamin, his other brothers and his father. However bad they may be, God can change anyone who is open to being changed, thanks to what Jesus has done for us all. And when this happens, a new person will replace the old one.

Credit where credit is due!

KEY VERSE

'Everything comes from him;
Everything happens through him;
Everything ends up in him.
Always glory! Always praise!
Yes. Yes. Yes.' Romans 11:36 (The Message)

WE ARE NOW back in the 13th century BC. Moses has completed his task and gone to be with God, leaving it to his successor, Joshua, to lead the Israelites. Of all the people who escaped from Egypt, it is only him and Caleb who have survived the forty-year trek through the wilderness and who will be entering the Promised Land with the next generation of Israelites.

Joshua has to work out a way to cross the River Jordan and take the land, but it is not going to be easy. The first problem is that he doesn't have a proper army, just a very large number of people who know all about wandering around a desert and sleeping in tents. The second problem is that the Canaanites, who are currently occupying the land, not only have experienced armies but also live in fortified cities, which somehow have to be captured.

Joshua sends out two spies to suss out the situation and tells them to concentrate especially on Jericho, as this is the first city the Israelites are going to come to. As they sneak in, the spies notice that Jericho has double brick walls, the outer one six feet thick and the inner one twelve feet thick. They also learn that the people who live in Jericho worship a fire god called Molek and a fertility goddess called Ashtoreth. Their dreadful and debauched rituals included child sacrifice.

The spies also find an unexpected ally, a prostitute named Rahab who lives right on the city wall. She lets them hide in her house and says she will protect them if they promise that the Israelites will spare her and her whole family when they attack. It seems that the people of Jericho and many others in the land are living in fear of the advancing Israelites. The stories of God guiding and helping them have spread far and wide. Rahab somehow knows that the God of Israel has already given this land – including Jericho – to them. She tells the spies she believes that He is none other than the God of heaven and earth.

The spies must be surprised to hear a prostitute say such things but they agree to her offer. She and her family will be spared as long as she ties a scarlet cord in her window so that the Israelites know where they are. She then helps the men to escape down a rope she throws down from her window. When they get back to Joshua, they tell him that the Israelites' reputation has already got the Canaanites terrified and, thanks to God, the land seems to be theirs for the taking.

Next morning, the whole nation assembles by the Jordan and is given instructions to follow the Levites, who will be carrying the ark of the covenant. The river is the one natural obstacle they have to overcome before they can get to Jericho; but God is there to help them and miraculously the flooded river stops flowing when the Levites carrying the ark reach it and so everyone can walk across on dry land. As Joshua approaches Jericho, he sees a man standing in front of him with a drawn sword in his hand. Joshua asks him if he is friend or foe and the man replies: Neither. He is the commander of the army of the Lord. Joshua prostrates himself before him and asks him what message he has for him. The man tells him to take off his shoes, as he is standing on holy ground. The last time anyone mentioned holy ground and taking your shoes off was over forty years earlier, when Moses was standing in front of a talking burning bush. On that occasion, God had given him his commission pre-Egypt. Now, Joshua is getting his commission pre-Promised Land.

The instructions Joshua receives are very strange. First, all his armed men have to march right round the city, once a day for the next six days, with seven priests carrying trumpets in front of the ark. On day seven, they are to march around the city seven whole times – and the priests are to keep blowing their trumpets the whole time! Finally, the priests have to blow a long blast and then all the people must give a shout. And then Jericho's walls will collapse and Joshua's men can rush straight in and claim the city.

As the Israelites proceed to follow these instructions, I wonder what the people of Jericho are thinking as they stand on their massive walls watching this bizarre behaviour. My guess is that, as they are already afraid of the Israelites, they find all this extremely intimidating. Finally, as the long blast of the trumpets sounds and all the Israelites shout, sure enough, down come the walls! But not all of the walls, it seems. Archaeologists have discovered that a portion of the wall on the north side of Jericho remained standing. Presumably, this was the part of the wall where Rahab had her house. This means it would have been easy for the Israelites to see the scarlet cord hanging from her window and make sure that she and her whole family were spared.

So, who was really responsible for the fall of Jericho? It would be interesting to have heard the conversations afterwards. The spies may have thought they were, as they got all the vital information on the city. Rahab may have thought it was her. If she hadn't hidden the spies and helped them escape, they would never have got back to Joshua with their report. Of course, Joshua had a large part to play in it. After all, he was in charge and it was he who had got the orders from the commander of the Lord's army. Maybe the seven priests who blew the trumpets thought they were responsible – after all, it was after their long blast that the walls fell down. What about all the Israelites' shouting? Maybe it was that that did the trick. And finally the armed men could have argued that they were the ones to walk thirteen times round the city and it was they who had rushed in and taken it. In truth, of course, they all played a vital part in capturing Jericho; but only one person can take the credit: God.

Today, I get a bit disturbed when people try and take some of the credit away from God just because He has chosen to involve them. Why does someone have to prophesy something personal at the front of a service when they could have had a quiet word in the ear of the individual or couple it concerns? Is it that they want the whole congregation to hear them so they can take a bit of the credit? (Of course, it's different if the prophecy is for the whole church.) Why does the person who claims to have a healing ministry say that people are healed as they pray for them? They seem to ignore the fact that those people's families and friends and churches are also praying for them and maybe it is *their* prayers God has answered. Are they wanting a bit of the credit?

Many times after I have preached I have prayed with people who have said they want to start a new life as a follower of Jesus; but I know that my input into their lives has been tiny. People have been witnessing to them and praying for them long before I came along – and I can't save anyone, only Jesus can. If afterwards I let people know how many people responded to my message, is it because I want a bit of the credit that is due to God alone? Although in His love and mercy He involves us in the work He is doing, we deserve no credit. Give credit where credit is due. All the praise must go to the God we serve.

❯ It's good news week

KEY VERSE

'How beautiful upon the mountains are the feet of him who brings good tidings, who publishes peace, who brings good tidings of good, who publishes salvation, who says to Zion, Your God reigns!' Isaiah 52:7 (Amplified Bible)

TODAY'S BIBLE STORY is set in ancient Israel in about 860 BC. What other things were happening around that time in other parts of the world? Imagine an evening late in the Greek Dark Ages, as a group of men, probably the wealthiest people in the community, settle down round the fire with a jug of good wine for a bedtime story. The bard begins a tale of the heroes of the Trojan War – an episode from the ancient Greek equivalent of a mini-series, so long it would have taken days.

Later Greeks believed that the greatest of these storytellers was a blind man named Homer who composed ten epic poems about the war and its aftermath, of which only two – the Iliad and the Odyssey – survived. However, modern scholars doubt that any such man ever existed and reckon that the works credited to him were actually created and assembled by many poets over many centuries. The only consensus is that both the Iliad and the Odyssey are landmarks in world literature.

But enough of Greece! Far more important, I hear you say, what was happening in Britain? Yes, of course … the mystery of Bladud. Almost everyone who visits the city of Bath will see King Bladud in his niche overlooking the King's Bath and will read the plaque proclaiming him the founder of that wonderful city. But who was he? Lud Hubibras (aka Bladud) was a British prince in Celtic times. When his father, King Lud, sent him to Athens to be educated, he contracted leprosy there and, on his return, his father disowned him and banished him.

Everywhere the prince went, he was shunned. He scraped a living as a swineherd, but things went from bad to worse when even his pigs caught his disease! To hide his disgrace, he drove them across the river Avon (at a place now called 'Swineford'), into the valley where Bath stands today.

One day, one of his pigs went crazy and rushed headlong into a black bog. Bladud struggled to pull it out and in the process became covered in the warm, foul-smelling mud himself. When he finally freed the pig, he found that the lesions on its skin had disappeared. ('Cured ham!' he thought …) Then he looked at himself and realised that where the mud had touched his skin, it, too, had been restored to health. Bladud immersed himself completely in the bog and was fully cured of the disease.

When he returned to court, he was welcomed with open arms by his mother, who recognised him by a ring she had given him. He became king and ruled wisely for twenty years. And as he knew he owed it all to the hot spring beneath that smelly black bog, he built a city around it in gratitude and called it 'Bath'. Is that a true story? I've no idea. Best ask a Bathonian!

But *this* story I know is true! The main characters are Elisha the prophet and Joram, King of Israel, who live in the city of Samaria. Joram persists in doing things that displease God and every time he does so, enemies rise up and attack his kingdom. We pick up our story in the middle of one of these bitter conflicts. Ben-Hadad I, King of Syria, has laid siege to Samaria with his whole army and the food is running out. The people in the city are so hungry that the butchers' shops are selling donkeys' heads (unclean for Jews) and even doves' dung for enormous prices! King Joram overhears two women arguing. They had made a deal and yesterday they had eaten one woman's baby as agreed, but now the other woman refuses to give hers up to be their next meal. The first woman appeals to the king for justice!

Joram rips his robes in distress and everyone sees that he is wearing sackcloth underneath. Sackcloth is very uncomfortable when it rubs against the skin and in those days it was worn as a sign of repentance. But this wicked king is not really repentant at all. He blames Elisha, because he prophesied that all this would happen. Joram vows he will have Elisha's head off by the end of the day and goes off to find him – and sends his executioner on ahead. Elisha knows that Joram and his executioner are on their way and he tells his servants to let no one in but the king himself. When Joram arrives, Elisha informs him that within a day the price of fine flour and barley in Samaria will plummet.

One of the king's officers sneers that he is talking rubbish, just trying to buy time. Even if God opens the floodgates of heaven and pours it down Himself, he laughs, it's never going to happen. Elisha tells him that he will see it for himself – but will not taste any of it. The king decides to let Elisha keep his head for another twenty-four hours.

Meanwhile, outside the city, four lepers really are starving. Given that they are going to die anyway, they decide to go and surrender to the Syrians – who knows, they might even take pity on them. At dusk, they enter the enemy camp and find it deserted. A miracle has happened. God has somehow broadcast the sound of a great army with chariots and horses and the Syrians, thinking that Joram has hired the Hittites and Egyptians to come and attack them, abandon their tents and make a bolt for it. When the lepers see everything they have left lying around, it's party time! They start eating the Syrians' food and drinking their wine – they even hide some of their valuables in case the people of Samaria come out and chase them away.

Nobody does. But then one of the lepers starts feeling guilty and scared. What if the people of Samaria come out tomorrow and find out what has happened? They're going to be punished! And, anyway, this is a day of good news and they're being selfish just keeping it to themselves. They must go to the city gatekeepers and tell them the Syrians have gone. The gatekeepers pass the message on to the king, who decides that it's all a cunning trap and while the people of Samaria are all scoffing themselves in the Syrian camp, their enemies are going to creep round behind them and take the city.

He tells his officers to find the last few horses in the city that haven't been eaten and sends two chariots out on reconnaissance. They drive as far as the Jordan and see equipment and clothes scattered all along the road. The Syrians really have run for their lives. The good news travels fast, and the minute the starving people of Samaria hear it they are pushing and shoving their way through the city gates to get at the food. Remember the officer who didn't believe God could do the impossible? Well, it just so happens that he is on gate duty and he is trampled to death in the rush. As Elisha said, he sees the food but never gets to taste any of it.

A cheerful story? Maybe not. But, as with all Scripture, there are lessons to learn from it. The thing that immediately leaps into my mind is the thought that occurs to the lepers as they think of all the desperate people inside the city: 'Today is a day of good news. Let's not keep it to ourselves!' Need I say more?

He ain't heavy, he's my brother

KEY VERSE 'This is how everyone will recognize that you are my disciples – when they see the love you have for each other.' John 13:35 (The Message)

A DISCIPLE IS a learner. A follower. An imitator of their teacher. Let's take a quick look at the twelve disciples Jesus chose.

Simon (or, more accurately, Simeon) Peter, son of John

Probably affected by John the Baptist, knowing the enthusiasm of his brother, Andrew. One of the three men in Jesus' inner circle. A fisherman. He is very outspoken and often acts first and thinks later.

Andrew, son of John

Brother of Simon Peter, and another fisherman. An ex-disciple of John the Baptist who, as soon as he meets Jesus, runs to fetch his brother. His faith seems to be very practical.

James, son of Zebedee

The second member of Jesus' inner circle. Another fisherman, who worked with Peter. Herod Agrippa I has him killed in AD 44, making him the first of the Twelve to be martyred and the only one apart from Judas Iscariot whose death is recorded in the Bible. He tends to be fiery and impetuous and lacks compassion.

John, son of Zebedee

The third member of Jesus' inner circle. Another fisherman who worked with Peter. His mother is Salome, the woman who accompanies the two Marys to Jesus' tomb (Mark 16:1). Many commentators regard her as the sister of Mary the mother of Jesus, which would make both James and John Jesus' cousins on His mother's side. His temperament is just like his brother's. Jesus nicknames the two of them 'the sons of thunder'.

Philip
Probably another ex-disciple of John the Baptist, like Andrew. He comes across as a sincere, approachable man but less of a leader than someone who can introduce you to the boss. He has no idea how Jesus could feed 5,000 people.

Bartholomew, also known as Nathanael
It is Philip who introduces him to Jesus, and as they are always mentioned together it sounds as if they are good friends. Nathanael comes from Cana, the rival town next door to Nazareth, which is why, when he first hears of Jesus, he asks sarcastically: 'Can anything good come out of Nazareth?' He's a bit of a cynic. He may have studied law and is maybe very narrow-minded, believing that Jesus should be interested only in the Jews.

Matthew, son of Alphaeus
A taxman, who would have become rich by ripping people off and would be barred from the synagogue and as despised as if he was a murderer or something. However, he leaves everything to follow Jesus and is happy to introduce Him to all the lowlifes with whom he has mixed. We have no idea about his personality, but we certainly owe him for writing the first book of our New Testament.

Thomas the Twin
We know little about him except that he is prepared to die with Jesus and is willing to admit that he doesn't understand what Jesus is saying. He finds the resurrection hard to believe, for which he has been unfairly nicknamed 'Doubting Thomas' – but when he finally meets the risen Lord, he is the first to realise that He must be God Himself. He is a loyal, down-to-earth kind of man and maybe a bit of a pessimist.

James, son of Alphaeus
Otherwise known as 'James the Less', to distinguish him from the other, more famous James. Maybe he is shorter or younger than him. He may be related in some way to Matthew and Thaddaeus. We know little about him.

Thaddaeus, also called Judas, son of James
Possibly he is the author of the book of Jude, which was written by 'Judas, a servant of Jesus Christ and a brother of James'. We know little about him. John's

Gospel, in its account of the Last Supper, refers to him as 'Judas (not Iscariot)'.

Simon the Zealot
A member of the fanatical nationalist group whose guerrilla activities are meant to drive the Romans out but instead just provoke bloody reprisals. He is, presumably, politically active and could be inclined to violence!

Judas Iscariot
'Iscariot' may mean 'dagger man' (or 'assassin'), meaning that he, too, is a Zealot, or it may mean that he hails from a place called Kerioth – or it may mean something completely different! If he came from Kerioth, he would be the only one of the Twelve who is not a Galilean, which would make him the odd one out. He seems to show signs of being a loner and misunderstood. The author of John's Gospel certainly has little time for him and refers to him as a thief, a traitor, possessed by the devil and 'the son of perdition'. Jesus trusts him with the little money they have and he becomes the treasurer. As for his personality, I'll leave you to work that one out!

In short, part of Jesus' core team includes two sets of brothers, possibly two of them His own cousins, and three others who seem to have been related somehow. These are the men He hand-picks to change the world! (And then there is **Paul**, a brilliant intellectual who is often referred to as 'the last apostle' as Jesus confronted him on the road to Emmaus. He describes himself as 'the worst of sinners', an arrogant man who at first insulted and persecuted the Church very zealously.) There may be some unlikely disciples reading this book, but when you consider the ones Jesus chose, there must be hope for all of us! Nonetheless, for all their shortcomings, all of them except Judas Iscariot lived up to their calling.
Jesus said: 'This is the cost of being one of My followers:
- 'You won't have a home.' Foxes and birds may have homes, but His followers must always be ready to move anywhere when He says so.
- 'You won't be around to bury your father.'(This sounds hard, but in Jesus' day many men would not leave home while their fathers were still alive. Jesus was saying: Don't follow Me when you feel the time is right; follow Me when I call you!)
- 'You will love others and care for them.'

- 'You will not love your father, mother, son or daughter more than Me, or put their interests before Mine.'
- 'You will take up your cross daily.'
- 'You will deny yourself and give up everything to follow Me.'
- 'You will listen to My voice and do as I say.'

As William Barclay writes in his Bible commentary: 'The Christian may have to sacrifice his personal ambition, the ease and the comfort that he might have enjoyed, the career that he might have achieved, he may have to lay aside his dreams, he will certainly have to sacrifice his will for no Christian can ever do what he likes, he must do what Christ likes. In Christianity there is always some cross as Christianity is the religion of the cross.'

Being an individual disciple of Jesus can be hard enough; but to be true disciples we have to learn to work with other disciples, and for some (as the original Twelve discovered) that can be *really* difficult. We have to learn to befriend people who may have quite opposite viewpoints to us. Matthew, the taxman, the collaborator with the Romans, love Simon the Zealot! Simon, love Matthew! We have to learn to love people with different personalities and characters.

'The wolf and the lamb will feed together.' Normally, a wolf would kill and eat a lamb. And this wolf is still a wolf – it hasn't been turned into another lamb. Nor has the lamb been turned into a wolf. The two creatures will be living side by side, however, and that means they will just have to learn to get on together.

So, to sum up. We must respect those who think differently from us and we must learn to work alongside other believers who have different personalities and characters from us. We cannot wait until people change and become the people we'd like them to be before we recognise them as fellow disciples whom Jesus loves.

'Blest be the tie that binds
Our hearts in Christian love;
The fellowship of kindred minds
Is like to that above.'
John Fawcett, 1782

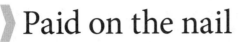

Paid on the nail

KEY VERSE

'But it was our sins that did that to him,
that ripped and tore and crushed him – our sins!
He took the punishment, and that made us whole.
Through his bruises we get healed.' Isaiah 53:5 (The Message)

I'M SURE MY old friend Graham Kendrick won't mind me borrowing one of his early album titles, but it's an inspired phrase that sums up this our last and probably most crucial study. It's so important to know what happened in the last few hours Jesus spent on earth, because it should make us all the more grateful for the love shown to us by our wonderful Saviour.

Let's begin with His capture in the garden of Gethsemane and the trial that follows. It is one big set-up between Judas and the Jewish religious leaders. After Jesus has been led away by the Temple police, it seems a strange coincidence that most, if not all, of the seventy-one members of the Sanhedrin just happen to be assembled that night. Jesus is taken to the house of Annas. The former high priest had been replaced by his son-in-law, Caiaphas, but he still wielded considerable influence. For sixty years, his family dominated the leadership of the nation, political as well as religious, as no fewer than eight of them held the supreme office of high priest. Annas asks Jesus questions about His disciples and His teachings. Jesus replies that He has done nothing in secret, so why is Annas interrogating Him? Surely it would make more sense to question one of His listeners?

It's at this point that someone smacks Jesus in the face for answering Annas in that way. Jesus responds that He has spoken the truth, so why did the official hit Him? Annas decides to send Him to Caiaphas, the current high priest. Joseph Caiaphas was appointed by Rome and it was he who made sure that Jesus was arrested, convicted and crucified by the Roman authorities. Annas had not sought to be popular with his Roman overlords, but Caiaphas would do anything to curry favour.

With no real evidence against Jesus, false witnesses are primed to make untrue accusations. However, these witnesses only contradict each other. One of the accusations is of blasphemy, but even that isn't valid, as claiming to be the Messiah doesn't constitute blasphemy. Caiaphas asks Jesus if He is the Messiah – and adds: 'the Son of God'.

Faced with such a direct question, Jesus has to say: Yes. But then He elaborates, explaining that one day they will see Him at God's right hand and coming on the clouds of heaven. This is just the sort of thing the high priest wanted to hear! 'Utter blasphemy!' he roars. He either seems to lose it at this point or he does a bit of the theatrical to impress the Sanhedrin members present. Anyway, he rips his clothes to show how distraught he is. No more witnesses are needed! The Sanhedrin all agree with him. Jesus must die.

Then begins the torture sanctioned by His own Jewish religious leaders. The Temple guards spit at Jesus and punch and slap Him. Jesus has a blindfold on and as they beat Him up they taunt Him: 'If You really are a prophet, tell us who just hit You!'

Then Jesus is sent to face the Romans. Pontius Pilate was Roman governor in Jerusalem for ten years. His power over everyone except Roman citizens in Judea was absolute. Historians inform us that he was proud, bad-tempered, obstinate and childish. He and Jesus were about the same age.

To appear before the Roman governor, the charges must be in some way political. If Jesus really is a threat to public order, it could look as though a rebellion is brewing – and that would be very bad news for Pilate in Rome. Three accusations are placed before him:
  • Jesus is perverting the nation;
  • Jesus opposes paying taxes to Caesar;
  • Jesus claims to be Christ, a king.

Pilate just doesn't want to get involved, however, and, as Jesus' accusers are the Jewish religious leaders, he is keen to see this as a Jewish religious problem. He knows that people in the Galilee area have been stirred up and, as Jesus is a Galilean and Galilee isn't part of his province, he suggests that He is King Herod's responsibility.

Herod Antipas was nasty! This was the Herod who, when drunk, had been tricked into having John the Baptist beheaded and he had a reputation for being lazy, vicious and extravagant. Jesus referred to him as a 'fox'. As it happens, Herod is in Jerusalem for the Passover and he is pleased to have the chance to meet Jesus, although all he really wants is to see Him do some close-up magic. Jesus won't even speak to the fox, even though the chief priests and teachers of the Law keep repeating their accusations. Herod, living up to his nasty reputation, just makes fun of Jesus – his soldiers dress

Him up in an elegant robe and mock Him. But Herod can't see that Jesus is guilty of anything, so he sends Him back to Pilate. Up until this point, Pilate and Herod have disliked each other but now they suddenly become friends. Maybe that's because they both feel the same way about Jesus.

Pilate tells the Jews to try Jesus under their own religious laws, but they reply that their laws do not entitle them to put someone to death. This is not true, of course. They could put people to death for breaking certain laws, but the difference was that it had to be by stoning. To fulfil prophecy, Jesus has to be 'lifted up' – which can only mean a Roman crucifixion. Jesus says nothing when He is asked if He is the King of the Jews. He knows that whatever answer He might give would be taken the wrong way. Pilate still cannot believe that Jesus is guilty as charged. The Romans have nothing against Him, and yet the priests are whipping up the crowd outside.

It was customary at this time of the year to release a prisoner. Pilate suggests that this could be Jesus, but this backfires as the crowd shouts back that they'd rather he released Barabbas, a convicted murderer. Pilate's intelligent wife now tells him that she has just had a very troubling dream about Jesus and He is innocent. Pilate is under huge pressure, as the crowd is getting hysterical. He decides to have Jesus flogged.

The Bible doesn't say how many strokes Jesus received. The Jewish limit was thirty-nine, but the Romans who were dishing out the punishment had no such restriction. The number of strokes would have been left up to the soldiers administering them, with the proviso that the victim had to be left sufficiently alive to feel the immense pain of the crucifixion that usually followed. Flogging was one of the Romans' cruellest punishments. The scourge had bits of bone and metal in it, and one kind, called 'the scorpion', had metal hooks in it which ripped off chunks of flesh.

Jesus, now very weak, is again brought before Pilate. He explains that His kingdom is not of this world and that He would have no power at all if God did not give it to Him. The crowd piles on the pressure by shouting that if Pilate releases Jesus, he will be letting Caesar down. Pilate shows them Jesus, covered in blood as He is, and says: 'Look! Here is your king.'

Now comes the ultimate blasphemy. The Jews hate the Romans and their emperor, but now they shout back that they have no king but Caesar! First they reject God's Son. Now they are rejecting God Himself. Pilate washes his hands, to signify that he himself finds Jesus innocent. Whatever happens to Him now is upon their heads. The crowd screams back, 'Crucify Him!' and

Pilate hands Jesus over to His fate. The trial is over.

But the ordeal Jesus has to suffer continues. Even more humiliation and pain are inflicted by the Roman soldiers, who are the masters of cruelty. A crown made of huge thorns is rammed onto Jesus' head in 'honour' of His Kingship. Weak through loss of blood, He is made to carry the crossbeam of His cross on His lacerated back, through Jerusalem and up a small hill. Finally, He is nailed up. The nails were blunt pins, carefully hammered in to avoid the main arteries (and a quick death). Anybody crucified was going to die very slowly, of exposure, exhaustion and, finally, suffocation. Jesus, God's Son, dies on the cross.

The Christian faith is the faith of the cross. It is built upon Jesus suffering and dying for us undeserving sinners. We preach Christ crucified, but we also preach Christ resurrected, as He came back to life two days later. So, we end not with sadness but with great joy and gratitude. The end of Jesus' life on earth meant the beginning of a brand new life that will last forever for those who believe.

Thanks be to God!

'We may not know, we cannot tell,
What pains He had to bear;
But we believe it was for us
He hung and suffered there.

He died that we might be forgiven,
He died to make us good,
That we might go at last to heaven
Saved by His precious blood.'
Cecil Frances Alexander (1847)

Index

NATIONAL DISTRIBUTORS

UK: (and countries not listed below)
CWR, Waverley Abbey House, Waverley Lane, Farnham, Surrey GU9 8EP.
Tel: (01252) 784700 Outside UK (44) 1252 784700

AUSTRALIA: KI Entertainment, Unit 21 317-321 Woodpark Road, Smithfield, New South
Wales 2164. Tel: 1 800 850 777 Fax: 02 9604 3699. Email: sales@kientertainment.com.au

CANADA: David C Cook Distribution Canada, PO Box 98, 55 Woodslee Avenue, Paris,
Ontario N3L 3E5. Tel: 1800 263 2664 Email: joy.kearley@davidccook.ca

GHANA: Challenge Enterprises of Ghana, PO Box 5723, Accra.
Tel: (021) 222437/223249 Fax: (021) 226227 Email: ceg@africaonline.com.gh

HONG KONG: Cross Communications Ltd, 1/F, 562A Nathan Road, Kowloon.
Tel: 2780 1188 Fax: 2770 6229 Email: cross@crosshk.com

INDIA: Crystal Communications, 10-3-18/4/1, East Marredpalli, Secunderabad – 500026,
Andhra Pradesh. Tel/Fax: (040) 27737145. Email: crystal_edwj@rediffmail.com

KENYA: Keswick Books and Gifts Ltd, PO Box 10242-00400, Nairobi.
Tel: (020) 2226047/312639 Email: sales.keswick@africaonline.co.ke

MALAYSIA: Canaanland Distributors Sdn Bhd, No. 25 Jalan PJU 1A/41B, NZX Commercial
Centre, Ara Jaya, 47301 Petaling Jaya, Selangor. Tel: (03) 7885 0540/1/2
Fax: (03) 7885 0545 Email: info@canaanland.com.my

Salvation Publishing & Distribution Sdn Bhd, 23 Jalan SS 2/64, 47300 Petaling Jaya,
Selangor. Tel: (03) 78766411/78766797 Fax: (03) 78757066/78756360
Email: info@salvationbookcentre.com

NEW ZEALAND: KI Entertainment, Unit 21 317-321 Woodpark Road, Smithfield, New
South Wales 2164, Australia. Tel: 0 800 850 777 Fax: +612 9604 3699
Email: sales@kientertainment.com.au

NIGERIA: FBFM, Helen Baugh House, 96 St Finbarr's College Road, Akoka, Lagos.
Tel: (+234) 01-7747429, 08075201777, 08186337699, 08154453905
Email: fbfm_1@yahoo.com

PHILIPPINES: OMF Literature Inc, 776 Boni Avenue, Mandaluyong City.
Tel: (02) 531 2183 Fax: (02) 531 1960 Email: gloadlaon@omflit.com

SINGAPORE: Alby Commercial Enterprises Pte Ltd, 95 Kallang Avenue #04-00, AIS
Industrial Building, 339420. Tel: (65) 629 27238 Fax: (65) 629 27235
Email: marketing@alby.com.sg

SRI LANKA: Christombu Publications (Pvt) Ltd, Bartleet House, 65 Braybrooke Place,
Colombo 2. Tel: (+941) 2421073/2447665. Email: christombupublications@gmail.com

USA: David C Cook Distribution Canada, PO Box 98, 55 Woodslee Avenue, Paris, Ontario
N3L 3E5, Canada. Tel: 1800 263 2664. Email: joy.kearley@davidccook.ca

For email addresses, visit the CWR website: www.cwr.org.uk
CWR is a Registered Charity – Number 294387
CWR is a Limited Company registered in England – Registration Number 1990308

Courses and seminars

Publishing and new media

Conference facilities

Transforming lives

CWR's vision is to enable people to experience personal transformation through applying God's Word to their lives and relationships.

Our Bible-based training and resources help people around the world to:
• Grow in their walk with God
• Understand and apply Scripture to their lives
• Resource themselves and their church
• Develop pastoral care and counselling skills
• Train for leadership
• Strengthen relationships, marriage and family life and much more.

Our insightful writers provide daily Bible-reading notes and other resources for all ages, and our experienced course designers and presenters have gained an international reputation for excellence and effectiveness.

CWR's Training and Conference Centres in Surrey and East Sussex, England, provide excellent facilities in idyllic settings – ideal for both learning and spiritual refreshment.

CWR Applying God's Word
to everyday life and relationships

CWR, Waverley Abbey House,
Waverley Lane, Farnham,
Surrey GU9 8EP, UK

Telephone: **+44 (0)1252 784700**
Email: info@cwr.org.uk
Website: www.cwr.org.uk

Registered Charity No 294387
Company Registration No 1990308

I Was Just Wandering

Jeff often describes himself as a Mr Bean of the Christian faith who has had more than his fair share of embarrassing mishaps and laugh-out-loud episodes. But in the midst of the laughter and tears, there's a lot to kick-start the heart and mind as well. *I Was Just Wandering* will help us to realise that we Christians all have thoughts and struggles that can taunt and torment, but this book will offer relief, and let us know that we're not alone.

ISBN: 978-1-85345-850-7

156 page paperback

210 x 210mm

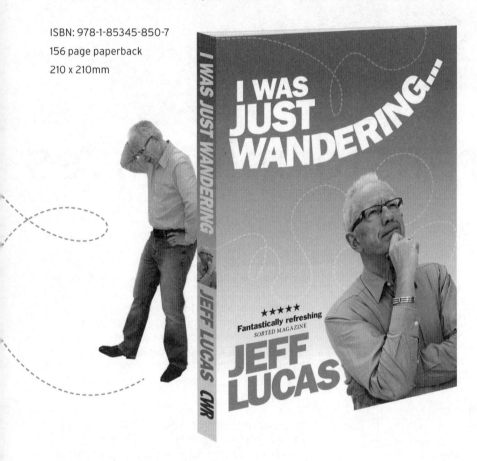

For more information and current prices please visit
www.cwr.org.uk/store